ESTABLISHED IN 1973

PUBLISHED QUARTERLY
by Berea College
CPO 2166
205 N. Main Street
Berea, KY, 40404

Telephone: 859.985.3559
Facsimile: 859.985.3903
Email: appalachianheritage@berea.edu
www.appalachianheritage.net

 Periodicals postage paid at Berea, Kentucky, and at additional mailing offices. ISSN# 03632318.

The short stories in this publication are works of fiction. Names, characters, places, and incidents are either the products of the authors' imaginations or are used fictitiously. Any resemblance to actual events, locales, or persons, living or dead, is entirely coincidental. The views expressed in the creative nonfiction herein are solely those of the authors.

Thanks to Barbara Kingsolver for her gracious permission to reprint the following:

"Where It Begins" first appeared in *Orion Magazine* (November/December 2013); "Ordinary Miracle" and "Waiting for the Invasion" first appeared in *Another America/Otra America* (Seattle, Wa.: Seal Press, 1992); and "Fault Lines" first appeared in *Frontiers: A Journal of Women's Studies*, Vol. 12 No. 3 (Winter 1992).

Electronic submissions only at www.appalachianheritage.net

Distributed by the University of North Carolina Press. Basic subscription price: $30/year for individuals, $40/year for institutions. For subscription requests and inquiries, visit the magazine's website, email uncpress_journals@unc.edu, or call 919.962.4201.

CONTENTS

BOOK REVIEWS

ILLUSTRATIONS

EDITOR'S NOTE

JASON HOWARD

In his poem "Digging," the Nobel Prize-winning Irish poet Seamus Heaney depicts a writer at his desk, a pen resting "Between my finger and my thumb," ready to begin his day's work. But the narrator becomes distracted by the sound of a spade striking gravel, and he looks out to find his father's "straining rump among the flowerbeds," digging away. The sight of his bent father floods him with a vortex of memory—of his father digging potatoes, of his grandfather cutting the turf of a peat bog, of the narrator himself carrying a bottle of milk to his working grandfather.

"But I've no spade to follow men like them," the speaker mourns, before turning his attention to the "squat pen" in his hand. "I'll dig with it," he concludes, a precise summation of the writing life.

Like the poem's narrator, the authors in this issue have chosen to excavate through their writing. They know how to handle a pen, using it to plough their memories, subconscious, and imaginations, tending to their vocation as faithfully as any farmer or field hand. And in this issue, they have gathered their harvest for us here, a farm-to-table gift for us to admire and savor.

As our featured author for this issue, Barbara Kingsolver has brought us a beautiful crop of writing and observations that spans literary genres. She starts with her essay "Where It Begins," originally published in *Orion Magazine*, and from which she read as part of her keynote at the 2013 Appalachian Writers' Workshop at the Hindman Settlement School, captivating everyone in the room. Kingsolver also contributes two poems, a short story that has not been published prominently, and a craft essay taken from an unpublished journal entry titled "Riding the Elephant." Finally, award-winning fiction writer Crystal Wilkinson interviews Kingsolver on her body of work, writing process, and deep Appalachian roots.

Also wielding their pens are Jordan Farmer, whose story "Lost in the Flood" was a finalist for the *CutBank* literary magazine's 2014 Montana Fiction Prize. Amy Clark, nonfiction writer and editor of the anthology *Talking Appalachian: Voice, Identity, and Community*, makes her fiction debut in this issue. Creative nonfiction writers Angel

Sands Gunn and Erica Langston contribute evocative essays. Joseph Banthanti, Marc Harshman, Amy Wright, and others burrow down deep in their poems. And acclaimed photographer Lauren Stonestreet provides beautiful visual context to our theme of digging.

Like the narrator of Heaney's poem, I hope you are carried away by these writings, transported to distant memories and places—and inspired to do some digging of your own. ■

WHERE IT BEGINS

BARBARA KINGSOLVER

It all starts with the weather. Comes a day when summer finally gives in to the faintest freshet of chill and a slim new light and just like that, you're gone. Wild in love with the autumn proviso. You can see that the standing trees are all busy lighting themselves up ember-orange around the hemline, starting their ritual drama of slow self-immolation—oh, well, you see it all. The honkling chain gang of boastful geese overhead that are fleeing warmward-ho, chuckling over their big escape. But not you. One more time, here for the duration, you will stick it out. Through the famously appley wood-smoked season that opens all hearts' doors into kitchen industry and soup on the stove, the signs wink at you from everywhere: sticks of kindling in the fire, long white brushstrokes of snow on the branches, this is the whole world calling you to take up your paired swords against the brace of the oncoming freeze. The two-plied strands of your chromosomes have been spun by all thin-skinned creatures for all of time, and now they offer you no more bottomless thrill than the point-nosed plow of preparedness. It begins on the morning you see your children's bare feet swinging under the table while they eat their cereal cold and you shudder from stem to stern like a dog hauling up from the lake, but you can't throw off the clammy pall of those little pink-palmy feet. You will swaddle your children in wool, in spite of themselves.

It starts with a craving to fill the long evening downslant. There will be whole wide days of watching winter drag her skirts across the mud-yard from east to west, going nowhere. You will want to nail down all these wadded handfuls of time, to stick-pin them to the blocking board, frame them on a twenty-four-stitch gauge. Ten to the inch, ten rows to the hour, straggling trellises of days held fast in the acreage of a shawl. Time by this means will be domesticated and cannot run away. You pick up sticks because time is just asking for it, already lost before it arrives, scattering trails of leavings. The frightful movie your family has chosen for Friday night, just for instance. They insist it will be watched, and so with just the one lamp turned on at the end of the sofa you can be there too, keeping your hands busy and your eyeshades half drawn. Yes, people will be murdered, cars will be wrecked, and you will come through in one piece, plus a pair of mittens. It's all the same wherever you go—the river is rife with doldrums and eddies, the waiting room, the plane, the train, the learned lecture, the meeting. Oh, sweet mother of Christ, the meeting. The PTA the town council the school board the bored-board, the interminably haggled items of the agenda. Your feet want to run for their lives, but your fingers know to dig in the bag and unsheathe their handy stays against impatience, the smooth paired oars, the sturdy lifeboat of yarn. This giant unwieldy meeting may bottom-drag and list on its keel, stranded in the Sargasso Sea of Agenda, but you alone will sail away on your thrifty raft of unwasted time. You alone are swaddling the world in wool.

Strangely, it also begins with the opposite: a hankering to lose time and all sense of purpose. To banish all possibilities, the winter and the summer, the bare feet under the table, the shattered day undone and dregs of old regard and bitter unsettled tea leaves and the words forever jostling ahead of each other in line, queuing up to be written. Especially those. Words that drub, drub, drub at the skull's concave inner wall. Words that are birds in a linear flock, pelting themselves in ruined fury all night long against the windowpane. Nothing can stop the words so well as the mute alphabet of knit and purl. The curl of your cupped hand scoops up long drinks of calm. The rhythm you find is from down inside, rocking cradle, heartbeat, ocean. Waves on a rockless shore.

Sometimes it starts terribly. With the injury or the accident or the wrecked life flung down like an armload of broken chair legs on your doorstep. Here lies the recuperation, whose miles you can't even see across, let alone traverse. Devil chasm of woe uncrossable by any known bridge. And in comes the friend bearing needles of blond bamboo—twin shafts of light!—and ombre skeins in graded shades that march through the stages of grief, burnt umber to ochre to gold to dandelion. She is not in a listening mood, the friend. Today she commands you to make something of all this. And to your broken heart's surprise, you do.

It begins with the circle of friends. There is always something beyond your beyond, the aged parents and teenager who crack up the family cars on the selfsame day, the bone-picked divorce, the winter of chemo, the gorgeous mistake, the long unraveling misery that needs company, reading glasses and glasses of wine and all the chairs pulled into the living room. Project bags bulge like sacks of oranges, ripe for beginning. Cast on, knit two together girlfriendwise. Rip it, pick up the pieces where you can, along the headless yoke or scandalously loose button placket, pick up and knit. Always,

There is always something beyond your beyond, the aged parents and teenager who crack up the family cars on the selfsame day...

you will have to keep two projects going: first, the no-brainer stockinette that can run on cruise control when the talk is delicious. And the other one, the brainer, a maddening intarsia or fussy fair-isle you'll save for the day when the chat gets less interesting, though really it never does. Knitting only makes the talk go softer, as long as it needs to be, fondly ribbed and yarned-over, loosely structured or not at all, with embellishment on every edge. Laughter makes dropped stitches.

It begins with a pattern. The arresting helical twist of a double cable, a gusset, a hexagon, a spiral, a fractal, an openwork ladder, an aran braid, a chevron and leaf, the eyes of the lynx, the traveling vines. The mimsy camisole you arguably could live without, the munificent cardigan you need. A mitten lost in childhood, returned to you in a dream. A pattern in a magazine, devised of course to tantalize. More embarrassing yet, the pattern hallooing from your neighbor's sweater while you're only trying for small talk, distracting you until finally you have to stop, apologize, and ask permission to stare and memorize the lay of her sweater's land. And once it all starts, there's no stopping. The frame of your four double-points is a sturdy raised bed from which you cultivate the lively apical stem of sock-sleeve-stocking-cap. It's all in the growing. From the seed of pattern, the cotyledons of cast-on, everything rises: xylem and phloem of knit-purl ribs, a trunk of body and branches of sleeves, the skirt that bells downward daffodilwise. You with your needles are god of this wild botany. It begins the first time you take the familiar map in hand, scowling it over with all best intentions, then throw it over your shoulder and head out to uncharted waters where there be monsters. Only there will you ever discover the promised land of garments heretofore undevised. Gloves for the extra long of hand, or short, or the firecracker nephew with one digit missing in action. Sweaters for the short-waisted, the broad-shouldered, the precise petite. Soon they are lining up, friends and family all covetous of the bespoke, because your best beloveds are human after all, and not off-the-rack. You can envelop each of them in the bliss of a perfect fit.

And a perfect color. It starts there too. Every eye has hungers all its own. The particular green-silver of leaves overturned by the oncoming storm. An alkaline desert's russet bronze, a mustard of Appalachian spring, some bright spectral intangible you find you long to possess. Colors are fertilized in-vitro with the careful spoon and the potent powder weighed to the iota, and born by baptism in the big dye kettle hauled onto the stove. Flaccid beige hanks backstroke listlessly in the boiling ink, waiting to be born again, until some perfect storm of chemical zeal moves them suddenly to awaken and drink down all the dye molecules in a trice. Like a miracle, the dark liquid goes clear as water before your very eyes. Afterward the damp yarn sings its good news from dripping loops in the laundry room, waiting to meet the pattern the wish the cool weather the living room the days-long patient fortune.

It starts with a texture. There are nowhere near enough words for this, but fingers can sing whole arpeggios at a touch. Textures have their family trees: cloud and thistledown are cousin to catpelt and earlobe and infantscalp. Petal is also a texture, and limepeel and nickelback and nettle and five-o'clock-shadow and sandstone and ash and soap and slither. Drape is the child of loft and crimp; wool is a stalwart crone who remembers everything, while emptyhead white-haired cotton forgets. And in spite of their various natures, all these strings can be lured to sit down together and play a fiber concerto whole in the cloth. The virgin fleece of an April lamb can be blended and spun with the fleece of a fat blue hare or a twist of flax, anything, you name it, silkworm floss or twiny bamboo. Creatures never known to converse in nature can be introduced and then married right on the spot. The spindle is your altar, you are the matchmaker, steady on the treadle, fingers plying the helices of a beast and its unlikely kin, animal and vegetable, devising your new and surprisingly peaceable kingdoms. Fingers can coax and read and speak, they have their own secret libraries and illicit affairs and conventions. Twined into the wool of a hearty ewe on shearing day, hands can read the history of her winter: how many snows, how barren or sweet her mangers. For best results, stand in the pasture and throw your arms around her.

Because, really, it does start there, in the barn on shearing day. The circle of friends again, assembled for shearing and skirting. One whole fleece, shorn all of a piece, is flung out on a table like a picnic blanket, surrounded by women. All hands point toward the center like an excessive, introverted clock, the better for combing the white fleece with all those fingers;

combing the black, fingers can see in the dark to pull out twigs and manure tags and cockleburs. White fleeces shaken free of second cuts, rolled and bundled and stacked, ready for spinning, look for all the world like loaves of bread on a bakery shelf, or sheaves of grain or any other money in the bank. The universal currency of a planet where people grow cold. On shearing day all ledgers will be balanced, the sheep lined up in the gates are woolly by morning and naked by night, as the barrows fill and the spindles make ready and warmth is bankrolled in futures. Six women can skirt a fleece in ten minutes, just enough time to run and collect the next one, so long as the shearer is handy. It starts early, this day, and goes long.

It starts in the barn on other days too, every morning of the year, in fact. The sheep are both eager and wary at the sight of you, the bringer of hay, the reaper of wool, as you enter the barn for the daily accounts. You switch on the overhead bulb and inhale the florid scents of sweet feed and hay and mineral urine and there they stand all eyeing you with horizontal pupils, reliably here for every occasion, the blizzard nights and early spring mornings of lambing. You hurry out at dawn to find dumbfounded mothers of twins licking their wispy trembling slips of children, exhorting them to look alive in the guttural chortle that only comes into the throat of a ewe when she's just given birth. The sloe-eyed flock mistrusts you fundamentally, but still they will all come running when you shake the exquisite bucket of grain, the money that talks to yearlings and chary wethers alike, and loudest of all to the ravenous barrel-round pregnant ewes. They gallop home with their udders tolling like church bells. In all weather you take their measure and send them out again to the pasture. And oh, how willingly they return to their posts, with their gentle gear-grinding jaws and slowly thickening wool under winter's advance, beginning your sweater for you at the true starting gate.

Everything starts, of course, with the sheep and the grass. Beneath her greening scalp the earth frets and dreams, and knits herself wordless. Between her breasts, on all hillsides too steep for the plow, the sheep place little sharp feet on invisible paths and lead their curly-haired sons and daughters out onto the tart green blades of eternal breakfast. It starts on tumbled-up lambspring mornings when you slide open the heavy barn door and expel the pronking gambol of newborn wildhooray into daylight. And in summer haze when they scramble up onto boulders and scan the horizon with eyes made to fit it just-so, horizontal eyes, flattened to that shape by the legions of distant skulking predators avoided for all of time. And in the gloaming, when the ewes high up on the pasture suddenly raise their heads at the sight of you, conceding to come down as a throng in their rocking-horse

Everything starts, of course, with the sheep and the grass.

gait, surrendering under dog-press to the barn-tendered mercy of nightfall. It starts where everything starts, with the weather. The muffleblind snows, the dingle springs, the singular pursuit of cud, the fibrous alchemy of the herd spinning grass into wool. This is all your business. Hands plunged into a froth of yarn are as helpless as hands thrust into a lover's hair, for they are divining the grass-pelt life of everything: the world. The sunshine, heavenly photosynthetic host, sweet leaves of grass all singing the fingers electric that tingle to brace the coming winter, charged by the plied double helices of all creatures that have prepared and justly survived on the firmament of patience and swaddled children. It's all of a piece. All one thing. ■

ORDINARY MIRACLE

I have mourned lost days
when I accomplished nothing of importance.
But not lately.

Lately, under the lunar tide
of a woman's ocean, I work
my own sea-change:
turning grains of sand to human eyes.
I daydream after breakfast
while the spirit of egg and toast
knits together a length of bone
as fine as wheatstalk.
Later, as I postpone weeding the garden
I will make two hands
that may tend a hundred gardens.

I need ten full moons exactly
for keeping the animal promise.
I offer myself up: unsaintly, but
transmuted anyway
by the most ordinary miracle.
I am nothing in this world beyond the things
one woman does.
But here are eyes that once were pearls.
And here is a second chance where there was none.

BARBARA KINGSOLVER

FAULT LINES

BARBARA KINGSOLVER

Randall is moving away from his living wife. With the reckless, innocent grace of a liberated animal he scrambles toe-and-hands up the face of a huge rock; this must be Africa because none of the trees look right. The two boys are little and hold onto her hands, watching their father. When he straddles the top Randall turns around to wave at the three of them. She's about to tell him to be careful, but then he jumps off, just jumps on purpose, as if he means to amuse the boys. It's much too high. His body bounces several times with a dull energy like an old tennis ball. He lies still, and then looks up at her sorrowfully because he knows he's going to die.

Grace wakes up with her breath quick in her throat. It's exactly five a.m. She gets up to check on the boys, who are breathing, as they've been doing steadily for more than a decade and will surely continue to do. She wishes she could believe it. Her new friends in California tell her to "trust the universe," but Grace sees nothing trustworthy about the universe; it's full of exploding stars. Randall didn't die in Africa but in Louisville, two miles from home, when a drill bit broke in the machine shop where he worked. His employer called it a freak accident. Grace considers it a freak accident that anyone ever makes it through life in one piece. When the life insurance came through she thought it would help her mindset to get away from Kentucky, so they moved to Oakland. Now she has earthquakes to consider.

She goes back to bed but sits up against the headboard waiting for the sun to come up and the boys to stir and another day to happen. The blue shirt she hugs around herself is Randall's, going threadbare at the elbows, wearing out without him. Maybe she dreamt of Randall out of guilt, because she's going on her first date tonight. A blind date; the term alone sounds hazardous. A redhead named Fiona in her Grieving Group is setting Grace up with her brother. Grace would rather pass, but Fiona has that California air of calling everything between here and New York "the Midwest," in a pitying way, and organizing your whole life for you over the phone before you know what's hit you. Fiona also likes to brag that her apartment is located exactly on the San Andreas Fault.

Grace's relatives have reminded her that Kentucky gets earthquakes too—in 1812 one hit that made the Mississippi run backwards. "There's nothing new under the sun to worry about," her cousin Rita declared. Grace is amazed at the things people will say, supposedly to be helpful. When she was pregnant, both times, women would stop her in the grocery to describe their own pregnancies, always disastrous. "Don't do what I did," someone actually told her once in frozen foods at Kroger's. "I went into labor in the fifth month and had a boy that's blind and retarded. He's at the Lexington Shriner's home." Grace was exactly five months along with Jacob then. It was Christmas Eve. She went straight home to bed, not daring to carry in the groceries from the car. When Randall got home the ice cream had melted into a huge puddle in the bottom of the trunk and then refrozen. He tried to make her laugh about it: he called it the Neapolitan skating rink. Randall always trusted the universe. And he ended up with a drill bit in his femoral artery. Grace wipes her eyes on his shirtsleeve. The people in her Grief Group say she's in the denial phase, but she's not denying anything. She knows he's dead. She just wishes she could go back and start life over. She'd meet Randall again and they'd move into a safe deposit box.

■ ■ ■

In the parking lot after work Grace has an attack of despair. Her job is not the cause. It's a position she secured with the help of her former boss, before moving here: she's a secretary for a company that sells High Pressure Liquid Chromatography systems to scientists everywhere. She's not clear on what High Pressure Liquid Chromatography is, but Kareema, the cheeky receptionist who shares the front office, has even less of an idea, and she's been there over a year. "Do I look like a rocket scientist?" she asks Grace.

She doesn't. She looks like an exotic paintbrush. She wears black tights and has dyed her hair fuschia on the ends and somehow persuades it to reach for the stars. She gives Grace wardrobe tips and tells her she envies her petite figure and undamaged hair. This is one more concern Grace hasn't much considered before: hair damage. When she confided this afternoon that she had a date after work, Kareema offered the loan of her lucky earrings.

So Grace has a pair of little silver snakes biting her earlobes now, but she has no idea what good luck would bring her, if she came into any. She doesn't want to drive to U.C. Berkeley and fall in love tonight. She wants to go home and find Randall in the driveway shooting baskets, missing on purpose so Jacob can win a round of Horse. Puberty is turning Matthew's face into an exact replica of his father's. He'll never even know what they look like, she thinks. When he died they still had pre-teen baby faces, no jawbones, no real noses yet, just stamped-out cookie-dough faces like all kids have till they've lived long

She doesn't want to drive to U.C. Berkeley and fall in love tonight. She wants to go home...

enough to reveal their family secrets. This revelation strikes her so hard she has to pull her car over to the side of the street and crumple around the pain in her stomach. She thinks of Randall's face in her dream, so pleased, before he jumped. Why Africa? Where is he trying to take her? How can she hold back what happens next? She lies curled on the front seat, staring up at the darkening sky and the reflection of a lighted sign nearby: a neon fish blinking its way to no particular reward. People have told her she's taking his death too personally. She wonders what options she has; if she were a plant, she'd take it like a plant. She sits up again, digs a Kleenex out of her purse, fixes her eyes, and drives.

Fiona's brother Loren turns out to be fortyish and tall, with long black hair and pale blue eyes and a blue tattoo in Chinese that curls around his wrist like a suicide scar. If you saw this guy on the street, Grace thinks, realizing this is a Kentucky girl's thinking, you'd expect him to ask for a quarter or steal your purse.But now here he is, her date.

Parking is a problem so they leave her car in his reserved space at the university and walk to the restaurant. Grace never knows what to make of Berkeley's cleverness: a stationer's shop called "Avant Card;" a coffeehouse called "Sufficient Grounds."

"In the town where I grew up," she confesses to her strange date named Loren, "nobody would even get these jokes." It's true. Grace barely remembers what she once expected to find here: trolley cars and the ocean. Now she isn't sure whether she's come up in the world or just moved to a city of pretenders. If these people have the answers, why are they living on a fault line? Also, they're dying like crazy: a great, sad wave of them. Loren touches her arm and they both stop to let a blind young man pass by—his sight taken, Grace now understands, by AIDS. She's learned about retinitis and pneumocystis and the other devastations from three different people in her Grief Group; she often feels she's being introduced to her new home through the tragedy channel.

They arrive at their destination, the China Doll. The menu is printed in Chinese with hesitant-looking translations in pencil. Grace laughs at an item called "Funny Tasting Eggplant."

"Who'd order that?" she asks Loren. "It sounds like you'd get salmonella."

He smiles. "My sister forced you into this, didn't she?"

"No, it's okay. She's trying to help me take charge of my life. She thinks I'm lonely."

"Are you?" Loren watches her. Up close he's going a little grey and seems more respectable than she'd first thought.

"No. I've got two boys. Did she tell you that? Teenagers in the house are like living in a buffalo herd." His face registers a tiny shock. People here always do that, she's noticed. It's one more backward thing she's done with her life, had kids before she was twenty.

"I'm envious," he says. "My life is too quiet. Nothing ever happens. Maybe one of my books might fall off the shelf."

Grace doesn't believe for a minute that this tattooed man's life is too quiet. It dawns on her that the envies people claim on her— undamaged hair, rowdy teenagers—are stretching it; they're just being nice to a widow from East Jesus Nowhere. She looks around the restaurant and wonders if everybody has already guessed this is a first date going on here. She and Loren are both practically glowing with miserable good will. "What kind of, what are you, at the University?" she asks. "Fiona said an associate professor."

"Of Chinese history," he says, and her eyes inadvertently go to his wrist. He looks down too, then draws up his sleeve and displays it for her. "It says, 'Beware of funny tasting eggplant.'"

Grace laughs, feeling grateful. Even if she never sees him again, she'll remember that he helped her get through this day. "So, can you read this whole menu?" she asks.

They're interrupted by a peppy blond waiter wearing checked pants and a moppy haircut something like Dennis the Menace. "Can I answer any questions for you tonight?" he asks.

"Sure," says Loren. "What is the meaning of life?"

"Enjoy it. You don't die with your assets, you die with your memories."

Grace is amazed. She doesn't think she'll ever be witty enough to live here. When the waiter is gone she asks, "What does it really say? Your tattoo. I'll bet it's some girl's name."

"Worse than that. It's a quote from the I Ching that I considered momentous when I was seventeen."

"You don't die with your assets, you die with your memories?"

"Something along those lines. Never get a tattoo."

The waiter brings their wine and they stare into their glasses. Then they both glance up as the blind man who passed them earlier comes into the restaurant with a companion and is seated at a far table. "Everything that happens to you is like a tattoo," Grace says quietly. "It might not show on the outside, but it's permanent."

"Or you think it's gone, but it comes back on you later," Loren says.

Grace wonders if he's thinking of AIDS. "You know what I keep imagining? Whenever I come over here to Berkeley I see all these guys blinded, in wheelchairs, and I think they're home from some war nobody knows about."

"Everybody knows about it, they just wish they didn't."

"No, I don't think so. There's lots of little towns like the one I grew up in where they're still just about totally in the dark."

"They haven't heard?"

"Oh, they've heard. But they scrub behind their ears and go to church and count on being saved. My cousin told me somebody I used to know was back there visiting his mother and went swimming at the Country Club pool. And after he'd left, the city council found out he was HIV positive. They revoked his mother's membership and drained the swimming pool."

Loren appears to choke, or laugh. "Drained the pool?"

"Yes. Can you imagine? They don't have any idea of how big a disaster it is. I guess they figure they had a near miss, but it's all under control now."

"People don't believe in disasters."

"I do," Grace vows.

"No, I mean real Cecil B. DeMille natural disasters, epidemics and floods and locust plagues. People believe in individual will. They think they can control what happens to them. Drain the pool, hell, drain the ocean. Uncontrollable pestilence and boils are things that happened a million years ago, to Moses, not to people who possess microchip technology."

"Right. Here's to pestilence and boils," Grace says, raising her glass. She's aware that this may be the un-sexiest conversation in the history of dating.

■ ■ ■

Matthew is asleep when she gets home, but Jacob is still up working on an experiment with goldfish he's conducting for a science fair. Grace is amazed at the difference between Kentucky and California school systems. Last year Jacob pasted photos of endangered species on a poster and won first prize; this year he's worked every night for weeks to make something Grace thinks ought to go on "Nova," and he says it's terrible, a lot of kids have better projects. It stuns her to realize she's brought her sons to a place where they'll grow up feeling second-rate, as she does. So many things in life she has failed to predict.

Adults walk around making jokes about global warming, even Jay Leno does, but Jacob looks up at the sky and chews the skin around his cuticles.

Jacob's experiment involves electricity, but he swears it doesn't hurt the goldfish. Grace believes it, because he's named them: Madonna and Goldilocks. Jacob has the softest heart of any fourteen-year-old she's ever heard of. He's been obsessed with endangered species all his life. Jacob believes in disasters, Grace knows. Adults walk around making jokes about global warming, even Jay Leno does, but Jacob looks up at the sky and chews the skin around his cuticles.

"They do this in Germany to test the drinking water," he explained to her on the day he brought home the fish and a box of electrodes. "They keep all these goldfish in a tank of city water downtown and they monitor the current. The fish give off so many electrical impulses per minute when the water's pure. If there's too much zinc or cadmium or stuff like that in it, then they give off less. It makes a power shortage, and that sets off an alarm at the headquarters."

Jacob's experiment only shows the electrical emissions from happy fish. His teacher told him he would need to show both control and polluted conditions for a chance at the prize, but Jacob said no. His room is papered with endangered cheetahs and great dying whales. He's not going to poison Madonna and Goldilocks with zinc.

■ ■ ■

On Saturday morning Grace feels an unsteadiness in her kitchen she suspects of being a tremor. Two minutes later the phone rings and she's pretty sure it will be Fiona advising her to go stand under a doorway. It's Fiona all right, but she just wants a report on the date. Grace runs down the details, including the menu of China Doll; there's not a lot more to tell.

"No electricity," Fiona concludes, and Grace laughs, thinking of Jacob's goldfish. Maybe we're swimming through too much pollution, she thinks, and then on impulse decides to tell Fiona about her dream. "Your brother's sweet, but I'm still too attached to Randall to see another man," she says, describing how her heart was pounding, how she woke up feeling guilty.

"He bounced when he fell? That sounds almost whimsical."

"It wasn't whimsical," Grace says, shocked. "It was awful. He looked down at us and then he just jumped. On purpose."

"Oh, I see what that's about. You're holding him responsible for his death," Fiona says. Fiona has been through so much therapy she feels qualified to say things that normal people would consider extremely none of their business. She and her husband got a no-fault divorce and lived for one year as best friends before he died of a drug overdose. This Grief Group is only the latest of a long series of Groups for Fiona.

"I don't hold him responsible," Grace says. "It was an industrial accident. I blame OSHA."

"But you blame him for being there. You've told me yourself you wished he'd finished his night courses and been a CPA."

Grace regrets bringing up the dream. She knows Fiona could be partly right. "I just feel abandoned sometimes. Not that it's his fault. I'm just, I don't know. Mad, kind of. It doesn't make any sense, but I'm mad that we got left behind."

"It's natural to want to blame somebody."

"I know. Your brother said people don't believe in disasters, they believe in individual will."

Fiona laughs. "Loren's a little intense. But it's true, it's the modern age, Grace, we all act like we were born with some certificate saying we're going to have perfect, happy lives, guaranteed. So if you slip on a bar of soap, you sue Neutrogena."

"I saw a show about that on *Oprah*," Grace says, hoping to change the subject. "This woman got window cleaner in her eye and went blind. She sued the window cleaner company, and then she turned around and sued her maid for taking the day off."

"It's a totally American phenomenon," Fiona says. "We refuse to accept bad luck."

■ ■ ■

After work on Monday, Grace drives into San Francisco to pick up Jacob from the science fair. Matthew will come home on the bus alone and log in a few more hours as a Latch Key Child. He's thirteen and seems tough beyond his years, with his spiked haircut and heavy high-topped sneakers, but Grace still worries.

"Mom, I think there's going to be an earthquake today," Jacob reports from the back seat as they're transporting Goldilocks and Madonna home. They won third prize. Grace is amazed and terribly proud of her son, considering all the competition, but Jacob seems subdued, taking in the day's news as cautiously as always, waiting for the other shoe to drop.

"An earthquake," Grace registers suddenly. "Why's that?" She doesn't doubt it a bit.

"All the experiments with white rats messed up today. They wouldn't go through the mazes or anything, they all just huddled up together in their boxes. It was lucky for me—that's the only reason I won a prize."

"You think white rats know when an earthquake's coming?"

"All mammals do. Except people. They can smell the positive ions that get released into the air."

"If that's so," Grace says, "they ought to have a big cage of rats downtown at the fire station, like your German goldfish."

"They do have rats downtown," Jacob says. "But nobody's keeping an eye on them."

Grace smiles. She believes Jacob is a near-genius, something she always felt about Randall too, even though he worked in an auto plant. He didn't want to be a CPA, he wanted to make cars. He just had his own crazy way of looking at the world. "So how come we can't smell the positive ions like other animals do?"

"I don't know," he says, and Grace can tell he's looking out the window thinking about this. They're approaching the eastbound on-ramp to the Bay Bridge. The double-decker traffic makes her nervous, with all those westbound commuters whizzing by above them, but her boys love crossing the water. She tries to relax and see the bridge as they do: an enchanted forest of I-beams.

Finally he says, "I guess we're tracking so many other stimuli that we don't notice the positive ions. We're too busy doing our own stuff."

Isn't that the truth, Grace thinks, and then suddenly her car is out of control. "Oh God," she says. "Oh my God, I've got a flat tire. I've got two flat tires." She pulls as hard as she can on the steering wheel and the car sways less and less violently and finally comes to a stop as far over to the right as she can get on the cramped bridge. She jumps out and looks under the car. She can't see a thing wrong with the tires on this side. She walks around to the other side, and then sees Jacob getting out of the car, laughing. He points behind Grace and she turns around.

A hundred other cars are pulled over, a hundred other drivers all bent over staring at their tires. It's taking everybody quite awhile to realize this isn't a personal problem.

She finds the scene hilarious. She thinks again of Randall, catching her eye, spreading his arms wide to embrace the air. It is whimsical; nobody knows what's going to happen next. That's where he was trying to take her—that far and no farther. There are only two choices in the "what happens next" department: to pretend it's your job to know, or admit you don't have a clue.

The steel cables over Grace's head hum strangely and then suddenly go slack. Somewhere the structure has broken. Lots of drivers have raised their hoods and are waiting for a tow truck, civilized salvation, hoping they still might make their appointments. For once Grace feels like the only person around who's getting the joke. It will be hours, if not tomorrow, before they're off this bridge. "Forget it, folks!" she says aloud. "Nobody's coming. This right here is the mess we're in."

The concrete is still trembling under her shoes and Grace laughs so hard she can't stop. There are stalled cars over her head and the dancing bay below and Jacob is hugging her. She decides to trust the universe. ■

WAITING FOR THE INVASION

In other years I watched the sky for birds
flying south in formation.
This year they pass in unbroken lines through my sleep,
driven down on machine wings.

I know the voice you use
for telling children not to fear
every droning sound
that scatters their play like shrapnel or shattered
ice across asphalt; every approach sends them
into piles of limbs under trucks,
sends the youngest under your breasts
that ache like the unmilked she-goat bleating somewhere,
ache with the waiting.

Every child has waited for death angels: I
listened at night for the Russians, who would
know our little town
by its twin water towers.
Someone, believe this, painted the towers black
hoping to save us.
And even now, fear is a night-time animal,
winged engines pulsing and the drone
of my mother praying
in the bed where she died.

No one slipped through a lake of night sky
in search of our secret towers.
No one. I know this now, but some believed
and believing still, prepare the massacre.

BARBARA KINGSOLVER

RIDING
THE ELEPHANT

BARBARA KINGSOLVER

A note from the author: *This is an extract from a journal I kept while I traveled through South Asia some years ago on a writing assignment. I always keep journals when I travel, because some of the information might be useful later if it's a research trip for a novel, or if I'm on assignment as a journalist. But I also do it because putting words to paper has always been* my way of *processing experience. I had no plans for this entry, I just jotted it down at the end of the day. Apart from one grammatical realignment and a tiny bit of context I've tucked into it, I surrender it here, unretouched.*

If it contains any revelations about craft, they might be about writerly habits, and going to the source. I had no audience in mind—it's a journal entry. But I'm surprised to see the level of detail, enough information to make the experience accessible to someone who wasn't there. That's habit, to pay attention to everything: sights, smells, sounds, physical sensations, the lay of the land. How can I say this? Writing involves no magic, only work. Attend, and translate everything into language as you go along. It becomes second nature. It becomes voice. It involves putting aside the self, and taking up everything else.

Another thing that surprised me here was the incipient presence of narrative. It's just a fragment, no real plot, but it does have a beginning and end. That, too, is a writer's habit. The difference between fiction and real life is meaning. The story has to tell me something, or it wasn't a story. Whenever some funny or appalling thing happens in my life, invariably someone says, "Oh, you'll use that in a story." And I think, no, I won't. Not unless, or until, I can figure out what it means. It takes certain writerly muscles to extract insight from incident, but those muscles get stronger with practice. After these many years I tend to see little narratives everywhere I look. —BK

■ ■ ■

After ten hours in a bus on the road from Kathmandu, I watched the steep, terraced mountainsides relax into the broad, flat plain that the Nepalese call the terai. The road followed alongside the river and bore the weary scars of heavy annual flooding, evidence of past springtime snowmelts from the Himalayas that swell this river to a hundred times its present, lazy size. Our bus bounced along the silty floodplain furred with maize and buckwheat, and intermittently passed through little plots of saal forest whose jungly wildness spoke of a Nepal I'd not yet seen. Mountains comfort me, and so do forests, but these were such a far cry from home. From the high plains we'd descended into the sub-tropics, home of elephants, rhinos and tigers. We were headed for the Chitwan reserve, an uncharted forest straddling the Indian border, one of the largest pieces of habitat the world has left for these and other Asian jungle creatures.

We entered from the northeast, leaving our bus at the park's edge because such traffic is not allowed. We hoisted our luggage and then ourselves into the back of a big, rugged truck that bumped over the rocky span of floodplain and then peeled right through the river's clear water. During the high water season, our driver explained, elephants carry visitors across. I couldn't imagine it. We checked into the lodge, a collection of thatch-roofed huts scattered through the jungle. Inside we found narrow cots, cold water and no electricity, camping accommodations, which seemed perfect in this location. I am a rural person; I felt at home. These few days in the Chitwan forest were planned as a respite after several weeks of hard work. My assignment, interviewing lowest-caste, so-called Untouchable women, had taken me into some of the poorest neighborhoods and villages outside of Delhi and Kathmandu. Which is to say, some of the most challenging places that any human on this planet calls home. Each day I'd awakened in a different strange room, trying to adapt to a kind of human crowdedness I had not previously imagined. Now I sat alone and inhaled the forest.

While we ate lunch, a Nepalese ranger arrived to say he was going to patrol the jungle along the park's northern boundary, the means of conveyance would be elephants, would we like to come along? There is only one answer to that kind of question. The four of us—my husband, two daughters and I—followed the ranger to the elephant-maintenance area. Without giving ourselves time to over-think this plan, we climbed the steps of a high platform and from there, carefully, as if getting into a boat, stepped out onto the large, table-like wooden saddle of our family's mount. Her name was Chichaankali. We sat down in the saddle facing sideways, two on each side facing out, holding onto the saddle's wooden rail, our legs dangling underneath it. The elephant's driver, a kid of maybe nineteen, sat on Chichaankali's head with one bare foot pressed gently into the flesh behind each of her ears, like the pedals of a car. He steered by pushing on one ear or the other. A chain that ran under her chin seemed to be the brake, as he pulled it sometimes with a "whoa" or a

We sat down in the saddle facing sideways, two on each side facing out, holding onto the saddle's wooden rail, our legs dangling underneath it.

sharp scolding. Our elephant was unusually distracted because of her eighteen-month-old son, who ran along beside us and sometimes nudged under her legs, wanting to nurse.

What a rocking, rolling gait an elephant has, like a horse galloping in very slow motion, but as much side-to-side as front-to-back. It's similar to horseback riding in the way that the body must learn to roll with the motion and lean forward on the uphill climbs. We passed through grass as high as the elephant's back, following the river, spying ducks and cranes along the water's edge. When we turned into the jungle, we quickly learned different riding skills as we constantly leaned and ducked to avoid tree branches.

But what a ride. We went for hours. As the afternoon deepened, our elephant lagged far behind the ranger's and we stopped at the river so mother and baby could take a long drink. Even through the wooden saddle I could feel our mount's huge lungs expand as she inhaled, sucking gallons of water into her trunk, and then the sharp exhalation and loud rush of water as she blew it from her trunk into her mouth, down her throat. The quantities involved are not sips but volumes, maybe about the number of gallons contained by the hot water heater in my home; the force of its movement I would liken to a fire hose. I had never paused to consider how much water an elephant trunk can contain. There is in fact a good deal of elephant anatomy one learns by sitting on its back, looking down at the feet, the coarse-haired flanks, the mottled backs of the ears. And of elephant murmurs, elephant talk. They speak to one another mainly by infrasound, a rumbling too low for humans to hear. From the lungs they set these vibrations into the ground, conducted through the feet I suppose, with sufficient force that their remarks can reach across many miles if necessary, to speak to other elephants at great distances. I had read about this, a fairly recent discovery by elephant scientists in answer to the old mystery of how elephant herds could know one another's whereabouts across vast areas, and convene at appointed locations. It is one thing to know the theory. But the first time I felt infrasound from my position on the animal's back, I registered it with some shock. It called to mind those vibrating beds called Magic Fingers that used to be in hotel rooms, rumbling up a massage for the price of a quarter. In this case, the price was motherhood. Every single time her baby strayed too far into the broad-leaved understory, Chichaankali let forth a magnificent rumble-rumble, and back to her side her bouncing boy came running.

There is nothing subtle about an elephant lolloping through a forest. Ahead of us, huge red and white cranes flapped away startled from their roost in a dead tree. Wild boars scuttled off noisily through the grass, and the jungle fowl—progenitors of domestic chickens—hunkered and scuttled away through the brush, eyeing us with exactly the beady resentment our barnyard hens at home cast toward passing cars in the driveway. We kept an eye out for tigers and did not see them, but the small hairs stood up on the back of my neck at the thought of these creatures sharing the forest with us, even invisibly. Especially, invisibly. The young driver was vigilant, the elephant even more so. It occurred to me that my touristic yearning to catch sight of a tiger was echoed by an equal and opposite yearning in the heart of the mother who carried us. We were all looking out for the tiger.

At dusk we returned, our mount slowing her pace along the cobblestone riverbank. The sky clotted with clouds that reflected in pink precision on the river's glazed surface. Jungle fowl crowed from the forest, a cockadoodle-doo so familiar it seemed impossible in this place. I held on to my ten-year-old's hand, squeezing it tightly, reminding her and reminding myself we were really here. We were riding through the wilderness of Nepal on the back of an elephant. Many times in the past two weeks I had second-guessed my decision to bring my family along on a work trip that had proven much more difficult than I'd expected. We'd been sick, afraid, weary, hungry, crowded, bewildered, and achingly sad in the presence of so many people with so little place for living. I couldn't say how many times I'd wished us all back home as I navigated those days, poised on the cusp of flight, longing to run away. And now I was so glad we had come this far. ■

AN *APPALACHIAN HERITAGE* INTERVIEW

BARBARA KINGSOLVER

In a world as wrong as this one, all we can do is make things as right as we can," Barbara Kingsolver wrote in her debut novel *The Bean Trees,* first published in 1988. Back then she could not have known that her entire ethos as one of our finest creative writers, public intellectuals, and humanitarians would be summed up in this statement. But consciously or not, that's what Kingsolver has tried to do time and time again in her award-winning works of fiction, creative nonfiction, and poetry;

in her advocacy on behalf of the environment, local foods, and social justice; and in her establishment of the Bellwether Prize for writers of "unusually powerful fiction."

A daughter of Appalachia who has lived and worked all over the world, Kingsolver has produced novels—among them *The Poisonwood Bible, The Lacuna,* and *Flight Behavior*—short story collections, essays, and poems that have been translated into more than two dozen languages. She has received Britain's Orange Prize for Fiction, the James Beard Award, the National Humanities Medal, and the Dayton Literary Peace Prize, as well as being a finalist for the Pulitzer Prize.

In a recent conversation with acclaimed writer and teacher Crystal Wilkinson, Kingsolver spoke of how her rural upbringing has "never left [her] psyche," finding her literary voice, and writing across genres.

■ ■ ■

CRYSTAL WILKINSON: As a child you grew up in Carlisle, Kentucky, and then lived briefly in the Congo. How did your sense of the outside world as a girl develop? How did it frame your identity as a woman and as a writer?

BARBARA KINGSOLVER: You've put your finger on the formative moment in my lifelong sense of place, belonging, and point-of-view. As a rural child in Kentucky, I claimed as my own universe the fields and woods surrounding our farm, and the few dozen children with whom I attended first grade. The next year my parents abruptly moved our family to the Republic of Congo, where my father provided health care to people who badly needed it. Instead of going to school I spent many months prowling with my brother around a village of thatched mud houses, no electricity or plumbing, no school, no stores, no roads or automobiles. We tried to befriend children who spoke no English and viewed our whiteness as a bizarre curiosity. The girls my age were all busy carrying younger siblings around as they fetched water, worked in manioc fields and gathered firewood from the jungle. Little boys climbed trees in search of things to eat, such as palm nuts or baby birds. I envied these kids' adult-like competence, and tried to keep up, but mostly failed. I accepted my status as an utter outsider.

Surprisingly, that stamp never left my psyche. When we returned to Kentucky I entered third grade and found that important things had happened in my absence. My peers had learned to fit their writing on one line of the ruled paper instead of two. Our segregated school had been integrated. Classmates sorted themselves wordlessly into groups based not just on skin color but also clothing, possessions, whether they lived in town or rode the bus—subtle supremacies that baffled me. The kids who were considered poor in our county were affluent compared with those I'd recently known, who literally had nothing but the shirt on their backs. I resisted the easy order, and fell into a gap that continued to widen. In small towns like these, all human interactions tend to begin with the unspoken question: *Are you one of Us, or one of Them?* I accidentally became Neither. I felt as if I'd taken an apple from the tree of knowledge, and gotten myself thrown out of the garden.

I did what lonely kids do everywhere (or did, before the internet): buried my nose in books about everyplace and everything, and made friends with other people who didn't quite fit in. Something in me was always watching life from the outside, permanently obsessed with the notion of belonging vs. not-belonging. It did not make for a happy childhood, but it was excellent training for a writer. At eighteen I left Kentucky and thought I'd never look back. I logged a couple of

Barbara Kingsolver

decades exploring the whole wide world, and along the way I began to see what I had loved about my childhood place, and how it might have loved me. I'd already spent years writing in journals, honing the habits of observation, so it was just in my nature to pay close attention to the nuances of language, culture, behavior, landscape, foods, scents, trees, the flowers that are in season—all the things that make a place what it is, and form the foundations for a person's attachment. If a sense of place is important in my writing, that's just my psyche. Place is the filter through which I understand everything. When I listen to conversations, I can't help pulling out the threads of idiom that are particular to a place. Over the years, as I've come to understand the poetry of the land that made me, I've forgiven its trespasses, and those of my own.

In my late thirties, when I could have chosen anyplace in the world as home, I chose a farm in southern Appalachia and moved back here with my family. The years since then have been the happiest of my life, and both my daughters have grown up with very happy, secure identities as Appalachian citizens. So my life and work have been a process of making peace with my origins.

CW: You were educated in biology before becoming a writer. How do these two worlds converge for you, both on the page and in your everyday life?

BK: I suppose I would say that natural laws are the ones I trust. I hold all human argument and hullaballoo in the context of a certain smallness: we're only one species, among millions. Every wren and groundhog and mosquito believes devoutly that its species—not ours—is the one that matters. I'm well aware of my dependence on other kinds of beings. Every breath I inhale was manufactured by a leaf; all that I eat was once alive, bent on its own survival and reproduction. Whether I'm getting up in the morning or sitting down to write, there's this understanding between the world and me that requires a substantial measure of humility.

CW: The UK newspaper *The Guardian* has described your work as "intently political and genuinely bestselling." I would add that you put the concerns of the world's social and environmental wounds in a lived existence in your books, most often through the bodies, hearts, and consciousness of women and children as characters. How do you manage to meld this research and politics with the concerns of the everyday lives of your characters?

BK: I manage it by paying attention to craft, only and always. I never ask any version of the question, "How can I wedge a political point into this scene?" It just doesn't work that way. I concentrate on character, theme, language, structure, voice. That's all. It actually surprises me that no matter what I write, people declare it "intently political." I'm just writing about the world I know, as it is. Wounds and griefs included.

CW: I read an interview in which you said that you began *The Lacuna* with a series of questions—that you were exploring why art and politics have such an uneasy relationship here in the States. Do all of your books begin with a series of questions? If so, can you talk about the questions that began your most recent novels?

BK: Yes, I always begin with questions. They are more nuanced than this, but for the sake of brevity I will simplify. *The Lacuna* began with my long-term curiosity about why people in the U.S. seem so suspicious of blending art and politics, compared with, for example, Latin Americans or Europeans who strike me as more comfortable with political art. I entered *Flight Behavior* with a curiosity about my own region: farmers around here already suffer damage from climate change, in the form of unprecedented droughts, floods, and tornadoes. And yet the people of southern Appalachia, on the whole, know less and speak less about climate change than more urbane folks tend to do. We're smart, thoughtful people. How can I explain this conundrum?

CW: Some of the writers you have said you admire are Toni Morrison, Gabriel Garcia Marquez, Jane Austen, and Kentucky's own Wendell Berry and Bobbie Ann Mason. Which writers—these and others—were most influential on your journey as a novelist? Who are you reading at the moment?

BK: Of the writers you mention, Bobbie Ann Mason especially influenced my roundabout journey home. After I left Kentucky, people mocked my accent, and shocked me with their "joking" presumptions about ignorant, unwashed Kentuckians. Without making a conscious decision, I retuned my accent and spent years trying to "pass" as a more urbane person. I wrote stories set in exotic places I had never seen. I would now describe these stories, categorically, as dreadful. After five or six years of this, a writer I knew from New York loaned me *Shiloh and Other Stories* by Bobbie Ann Mason, and it knocked me out. Mason had this quiet, utterly confident voice that even sophisticated New Yorkers admired, and Mason was a Kentuckian. Unapologetically, a Kentuckian. For the first time, a voice behind my ear said, "Stop pretending. Find that place down inside that's really you, and write from there." Within a few months I'd written *Homeland* and

Barbara Kingsolver accepting the the 2010 Orange Prize for *The Lacuna*.

Rose-Johnny, which I consider the first bearable fiction of my career. Then I lit into *The Bean Trees* with the feeling that I'd found my voice and hit the gas. I guess the rest is Kentucky Girl History.

Some recent reads that have moved me immensely are Alice Munro's *Dear Life,* and *Independent People,* by the Icelandic Nobel Prize-winner Halldor Laxness. The latter is as Appalachian a book as ever I've read, despite its setting in nineteenth-century Iceland. And I also want to mention the remarkable play, *This Is My Heart for You,* by Silas House. Ever since I read it, I'm longing to see it staged.

CW: You're most widely identified as a novelist, so some readers don't realize that you have often crossed genres, writing creative nonfiction essays and poetry. Is writing outside of your home genre of fiction a challenge, or do you find it liberating?

BK: Really I feel equally at home in fiction or creative nonfiction. I worked for years as a journalist, and I started keeping a diary at age eight, so it seems like a relatively recent innovation to declare myself a novelist. The basic techniques of fiction and creative nonfiction feel so similar to me, it's no stretch at all. Now, poetry is another matter. Poetry feels like a country I visit without a passport, where I look around furtively, grab hold of something precious, and try to smuggle it back across the border. Any poem I get written down feels like contraband to me.

CW: A friend of mine says, "If you want to know how to access the power of verbs in your scenes, go read Barbara Kingsolver." I agree and often use your work in teaching students about the craft of fiction writing. What insight

might you have for a writer who looks to your work to learn something about the writing process and becoming a better writer?

BK: I offer this insight: root out all the "to be" verbs in your prose and bludgeon them until dead. No "It was" or "they are" or "I am." Don't let it be, make it happen.

This insight took root in my soul in the following manner: after I earned my graduate degree in biology I took a job as a scientific writer for the University of Arizona. I spent my days reading reports of scientific research, and translating them into material that ordinary citizens (non-scientists) would want to read. Such leaden barges of verbiage oppressed me, I can hardly bear the recollection of those years. Honestly, after every few pages of Science I wanted to crawl under my desk and take a nap. But I love science! So why, I wondered, is all this prose so stupefying? How can these educated, articulate men and women of science all speak in the same soporific tongue? And then the problem dawned on me: the passive voice! The parameters are described...the results are found. Zzzz. Were these writers purposefully concealing the business of who actually did the work, and what they actually did? No, they couldn't help it, they had to write that way. But I did not. So I learned how to burrow into every passive and render it an active. For reports that crackled and sparked instead of falling over dead, I learned to supply the secret ingredient: verbs, in varieties infinite and endless. ■

FALLING WATERS
UNDER THE CITY GEOCACHE

Nashville Public Square
parking garage waterfalls—
a Green Roof Award

for harvesting rain, hosting
picnics, concerts, second dates,

an oft-overlooked spot
where city planners preserved
underground water

currents, integrated park,
seep, Ford, Toyota, Volvo,

pigeon coos and stone
profiled time, wildcat sirens
plummeting from the

Courthouse, pedestrian gush
over historic markers:

1714
The only white resident
in 12,000 years

set up a river station,
procured bear pelts from natives:

Circa 1000
A.D., Woodland Indians
cultivated bean

seeds, corn to augment forage—
a prehistorical peak

in development
evidenced by jewelry,
pipes, combs—a complex

territorial people
eroded by manufacture,

guns, foreign germs, myths.
There is no paradise but
self-sufficiency.

In 1748
160,000

deer, river otter,
beaver skins left on pack trains—
wild man-made profit.

Rivers felt boats of hollowed
alder, lime-snared birds, dripping

trawl of nets, wood split
with wedges, then iron, until
each cornfield became

labor. Toil mastered every
thing, relentless toil, tillage...

But now—we tuck signed
guitar picks in rusted bike
locks, pile sand dollars

beneath Chet Atkins statues,
squirrel nuts for others to find

in safe deposit
boxes, public offices
we hold an instant

then turn over, give ourselves
a reason to go anywhere,

be here, where someone
has been before, everywhere
before. Renew our

potential to scavenge up
something from found packages

of heirloom pea seeds.
Stranger whose real-time capsule
I fondle, to you

I leave a photograph of
Eustace and Winnie taken
here in 2000.

Outlined in organdy, she
leans over the rail, tip-toed

in heels, outreaching
one finger to the weeping
wall, drizzle of iron,

en route to the symphony,
one sepia strand of hair

undone in exhaust
scented air. One hand on her
hip, pussy willow

grey eyes in the headlight wash
looking two hundred feet up.

On the back in wax
pencil: "For all such things left
intentionally."

Find out why this place is so
special, photograph yourself

standing by the North-
West elevator waterfalls,
measure the stream mag.

using the chart provided.
Magnitude is measured by

discharge, 1 being
largest, 0 being no
flow or historic flow. Thank you.

AMY WRIGHT

* Italicized lines adapted from Virgil's *The Georgics.*

THE APPLE

People drank the apples John "Appleseed" Chapman
planted during his Ohio migration

to Marietta by catamaran his scattered orchards slated
to be hatcheted in the name of Prohibition

before the Women's Christian Temperance Union
repositioned the Hard Cider Nation, traded

knock-down drag outs for blossom-punched pie safes.
Cure-alls, they called them, rewriting the story

of the vegetarian eccentric *who once punished his foot*
for squashing a worm by throwing away his shoe,

wintered in a carved-out sycamore
outside Defiance likened his ways to a bumblebee's,

lashed a side car of moss-cloaked seeds
to his hollowed hickory canoe—

Malus domestica
from *Malus sieversii,* wild sour fruit from the Old World

botanists have traced to Kazakhstan—
died wearing a coffee sack *leaving a 1,200 acre estate,*

snake root and joe pye weed trail sentries, first waft
of seasonal shift in the swamp gas, death

come to the luna moth he woke to find   on his chest, silk-soft
dust of her scales under fingertips   and himself

bathing in Little Soddy Creek   losing his matte finish
of pollen drift   a bobcat-stalked piss, nubby crow's feet

carpet in which he washed   apple-fleck-sized spears
from prickled hands   looking

into a night sky   stars not white but red,
green-white   fleabane-colored, yellow

at the center with lavender edges   if he kept his open eyes
fixed   on nothing, his dust body wet.

AMY WRIGHT

LOST
IN THE FLOOD

JORDAN FARMER

Zachary's mother spent all morning on Mrs. Crawford's hair and that evening they laid her out in the viewing room for the mourners to pass by. People complemented his father on the fabricated vitality in her cheeks, the shine of life painted on the cold skin. Zachary stood by listening as long as he was able, then sat outside on the deck watching the news vans parked across the street. The men from the city leaned against the door panels sipping coffee from Styrofoam cups. Their suits looked too tight, the fabric's sheen glistening in the setting sun as they unpacked their equipment in hopes of getting a photo of Brother Crawford and his snakes.

Days before, Zachary's father had explained the service would bring attention. Zachary almost asked if he still had to work the funeral, but knew it would only make the old man angry, like the time he opened the morgue door and had nightmares for a month after seeing Rachel Marcum on the slab. That gapping Y incision, the deflated balloons of her lungs.

A few of the bereaved came outside to smoke and chat. They smiled at Zachary with their false teeth, wrinkled hands trying to get matches struck in the hard wind that blew the dying fibers of their hair. Some touched his padded shoulder and told him he looked very dignified in his suit and tie. Old ladies thanked him for escorting them to their seats. Still, conversation was more forced than at other wakes. Zachary worked enough to know that most people treated funerals as a social event. Mourning was really for the immediate family and a brief moment of sorrow in front of the casket. The rest of the time was for backslapping and hellos, jokes told outside the parlor while men sipped white lightning from flasks. His father told him this was normal, it was the way men dealt with knowing one day they'd too be laid out up front, but these men couldn't seem to shake that feeling. After a moment of camaraderie, the smiles slipped away and they stood solemn. When they finally spoke, the men only managed hollow things like "Undertaker sure did a good job."

Zachary knew his father's labor hadn't been easy. The night they brought the body, his father had gone downstairs to look at the damage. Zachary was supposed to be in bed, but he slipped out and listened to his parents talking hushed in the kitchen's darkness. His mother's voice rattled with the husk of sleep and his father's words carried their Saturday night beer burden, as if his tongue needed to whittle each phrase down into something he could spit out.

"Hands are the worst. Swollen twice the size," he said. "Skin burst in some places."

"Is that where..."

"I'd say so. Got her on the neck once, too. Michael said it was like a frog, but the church type will want her in something high collared anyhow."

"How many times?" His mother seemed afraid of the question. Asked it the way she asked about bills.

"At least three."

"Jesus," his mother said.

"You need to be prepared," he told her. "The kind of crowd that's coming will draw the media." His father said media with the same tone reserved for other hated parties likes politicians, poachers, and scabs.

The mourners on the porch looked ready to fight the camera wielding outsiders. Bill Payne, one of Lynch's oldest residents who seemed to be kept aloft only by his cane, pointed a crooked finger toward their vans as he pontificated on the wickedness of such a profession.

"Man makes his money taking pictures of someone's grief ought to be shot," he said. "If the world's going this way, I believe I'd rather be lying up there beside Jenny." He turned to Zachary and offered him a cigarette.

"Please," Zachary said. He took the man's Zippo and lit it. One of the men across the street raised his camera and snapped a picture. Zachary rose, ready to go take the camera away, but Bill laid a hand light as a turkey feather on his shoulder to keep him down.

"Leave it," he said. "All mountain men end up a spectacle eventually."

Zachary guessed it might be true, but it didn't keep him from stewing on it. He didn't like the idea of being watched, the feeling of being a spectacle for others. He smoked the cigarette down until the cherry warmed his knuckles and then pitched it into the lot.

Down the street, Fenton Collins came toting a flour sack in front of him. His patched jeans were speckled with mud and the Carhartt work coat he wore was at least one size too big for him, the sleeves devouring his hands until only the fingertips grasping the bag were able to peek out. His hair

He didn't like the idea of being watched, the feeling of being a spectacle for others. He smoked the cigarette down until the cherry warmed his knuckles and then pitched it into the lot.

looked as if he'd styled the long curls with dirt instead of pomade. The men next to the vans all turned their attention towards him, but none snapped a picture.

Zachary and Fenton went to school together until Fenton dropped out in the fifth grade. The principal had threatened to sick the truant officer on him, ship his ass up to Pruney Town, but Fenton wasn't the sort that could be caught. He and his father lived in a trailer on the hillside, and folks said his whole family lived wild. Talking with Fenton always made Zachary uneasy. Seeing the boy's days of dirt made Zachary aware of his clean nails, his polished if hand-me-down wingtips and his wool suit jacket.

Fenton stood at the foot of the patio steps, but didn't ascend.

"Evening," he said. "I got business with the bereaved."

"Brother Crawford's inside right now," Zachary said. "Can you come back?"

"He asked me here. Would you mind fetching him?"

Bill turned and started inside on his cane, each step a slow and calculated shuffle. Age wasn't the only thing that slowed his stride. Zachary had seen him kick his shoes off and show the holler boys the nubs of toes eaten by frost bite in Bastogne during World War II.

Fenton spit between his own shoes and sat the sack against the ground. Zachary noticed it was shifting, something inside writhing now that it rested on the asphalt.

"What's inside?"

"Come closer," Fenton said.

Zachary walked down the steps. The wind came down harder, making him stagger until he reached out and braced himself against the aluminum pillars of the patio. A soft shutter emitted from the bag that was barely heard over the breeze.

"Look," Fenton said. He opened the bag so Zachary could lean over it and peer inside.

The canebrake rattler was coiled three times in a circle, head raised and tongue flicking in hopes of tasting freedom. Its rattle was high and singing, a sound like snow on the television.

"Jesus," Zachary said and stepped back.

Fenton chuckled and closed the sack back up.

"Must be fifteen feet long," Zachary said. "What in hell are you doing with that?"

"It's for the preacher," he said. "Gonna get a hundred dollars for him."

Zachary had never heard of someone fourteen making that kind of money for a day's labor. His father paid him nothing for his work at the funerals, but he supposed he didn't really need any compensation. His parents bought him any necessities, the occasional want from time to time. Still, he envied the idea of Fenton making money selling snakes to the preacher. It seemed a proper job for a man. Better than ushering old woman and wearing itching wool coats.

"I could use a partner," Fenton said as if he could read the money lust on Zachary. "Cut you in for thirty percent."

"Don't seem like a fair shake."

"Gotta raft down Cow Creek to get them. I'm the one with the raft."

"What kind of boat could you have?" Zachary asked.

"Ain't a boat. Old top for a truck bed. Sealed the holes and she floats just fine."

It was hard for Zachary to imagine such a vessel navigating the water, but if anyone was capable it was Fenton. The boy had always been the kind to make do.

Moans sounded from the steps behind him and Zachary turned to see Brother Crawford descending the steps. He wore a black suit with sleeves an inch too short, a white shirt buttoned at the collar without a tie. Rumor was those sleeves covered a series of scars from the eight or so bites he'd received while pastoring The Holy Ghost Church of Christ, the last of the serpent carrying flocks in the southern part of West Virginia. Crawford stopped next to Zachary and gave a weak smile, gaunt cheeks hollow as a carved pumpkin and still carrying their constant look of agitation.

"That for me?" he asked and pointed a finger with scarred and bulbous knuckles at the sack.

"Yes, sir," Fenton said.

The preacher dug a single bill from his slacks and handed it over. Fenton deposited it inside his shirt pocket.

"My condolences," Fenton said.

"She died in the grace of the Lord," Crawford said. "That's all that matters."

Crawford leaned over the bag and peered inside, his face changing for the first time to something resembling pleasure.

It was an odd transformation, as if Zachary were watching the preacher's bones shift under the tight skin. The snake still sang inside the bag.

"You boys watch," Crawford said. "I shall show you the faith that spared Noah from the flood."

He reached inside and came out with the serpent held aloft, the long body shifting and curling around his cupped hands. The preacher began to kick his booted feet, to shuffle about in the dusty lot in a bizarre dance with the snake leading. He spun and turned towards the cameras letting the snake's tongue flick obscenely at the men. Zachary watched as cigarettes and Styrofoam cups were discarded and the flashing

Crawford leaned over the bag and peered inside, his face changing...It was an odd transformation, as if Zachary were watching the preacher's bones shift under the tight skin.

bulbs lit up the dusk. Cold coffee puddled around the men's expensive shoes.

"This is it," Crawford bellowed and his voiced filled with a holy haunt. "This is how to be delivered."

Zachary and Fenton watched, both transfixed and frightened, but neither denying the power of the transformation. The preacher held the snake aloft and his body shook, a tremor running down his extended arms and through the rest of him as if the serpent were a direct conduit to the eternal. His mouth babbled, spittle flecking from his lips, speaking nonsense or truth only he could understand.

■ ■ ■

After the proceedings ended, Zachary's father cleaned up the viewing room where a few guests had left snotty napkins or peppermint wrappers littering the floor. Zachary assisted, but had trouble focusing with Mrs. Crawford still up front. The lid was closed on the casket, but he couldn't stop thinking that the next day she would be carried to the private family plot and laid in the earth with the tree roots. He kept picturing the preacher dancing with the snake, joy filling him despite his wife's body being just inside. He wondered how it was possible. So many men he knew were beaten by country life, drowning in drink and popping pills that it was strange to see a man believe in anything. Most on the mountain followed a religion of mistrust, a fatalistic belief that the next day would be the same as before. How could the preacher carry faith, especially when the faith had robbed him of his wife? Zachary decided the answers were beyond him and continued to pick up trash.

After they finished cleaning the viewing room, Zachary took out the garbage with his father. He was hefting the first bag into the dumpster when his father spoke up.

"I want you to give the preacher a wide berth."

"How come?" Zachary asked.

"A man who tempts the Lord, especially right after his wife died from such foolishness, that's a dangerous man. Lord gave us fear for a reason. You understand?"

"Yes, sir."

"Good." His father patted his back and went upstairs. Zachary stayed outside, smoked the last of a stolen cigarette from a funeral guest, and thought about Old Lady Crawford. He decided he needed to see. After the smoke was spent, he walked quietly across the wooden floor of the viewing room to the coffin. It took him a moment to find the resolve to lift the lid, but once she was exposed he understood why his father had worked so hard to keep him occupied and away from a clear view of the body. The hands were packed into nearly transparent white dress gloves like too much meat into the skin of a sausage. Even with the layers of thick foundation, he could see the purple hues her skin had changed to before she passed, and under the high collar, a bullfrog neck.

Zachary considered Fenton and his snakes, the way he'd carried the bag as if it wasn't filled with death. He wasn't sure if he respected the boy or found him stupid, but he knew that he envied the sort of fortitude it took. He closed his eyes and tried to imagine the weight of a snake in his hands, the prickling of the scales on his palms as he began to shuffle up and down the aisle, twisting in a perverse tango with the imaginary serpent coiling around his thin wrists.

■ ■ ■

He went to Fenton's three days after the funeral. Fenton sat outside, his hat pulled over his eyes and his feet, stuffed into last year's boots that had grown visibly tight, propped on an old stump. Zachary admired the leisure. His back was sore from his pallbearer duty of carrying Mrs. Crawford up an overgrown hill to her family plot and his fingers were calloused from gripping the brass handrail. Fenton didn't look up as he approached, so Zachary gave his feet a friendly kick.

Fenton removed his hat. "You'd have been gutted with my Case knife if you were anyone else."

"Good thing I ain't."

Fenton spit at a nearby pine. "What's up?"

"I was wondering if that offer still stood."

"Snake hunting?"

"That's the one."

"Yeah, the preacher said he could use a few more for the congregation. Rattlers are his preference, but I know where we can find a copperhead or two he's likely to want."

"Sounds good. When do you wanna leave?"

"I ain't occupied," said Fenton. "Let me get the gear."

Zachary waited outside while Fenton retreated into the small trailer he and his father occupied. It was a rusted out piece of scrap, places being eaten away by age until Zachary guessed he could poke fingers through the weak membrane of the steel. The windows were covered in boards on the outside and a smell emitted from the open doorway like fried chicken left for days on the counter. Fenton came out carrying two metal poles with hooked ends. He passed one to Zachary and stood using the other like a cane. It made him resemble a wise man in a Christmas pageant.

"Here," Fenton said. "Others got the Lord with them. I'll trust the stick."

He pulled a flour sack from the deep pocket of his camouflage overalls and handed it to Zachary.

"Let's head out."

The raft was worse than Zachary anticipated. Nothing more than a fiberglass cover for the bed of a truck, the rectangular shell too tall and flat in the front to cut easily through the water. Zachary walked around it while Fenton grabbed a corner and pulled it down the bank into the shallows. Watching the muddy water cover the boy's shoes disgusted Zachary. Some people who lived on the creek dumped garbage after a solid rain raised the water level a few feet. The water looked higher than usual, the normally wide banks submerged until the swell almost swallowed the weeds that flanked the hillside.

"Ain't even had my tetanus shot," Zachary said.

"I figure we go down river a few miles, hit the sweet spot I found, then just ride the flow on down to the church," Fenton said. "It'll likely be dark, but Crawford will be there."

“Have you went that far downriver before?” Zachary asked.

“Not that far, but it’s only another mile or so.”

Fenton loaded their raft. He tied the snake poles down with bungee cords so they wouldn’t roll about when they hit hard water and offered Zachary his hand. Zachary climbed aboard while Fenton put his foot into the weak bank and shoved off. The truck top drifted easy on the current, a surprisingly smooth ride with the rocks only scraping and pinging against the bottom of their hull. Zachary stayed in the middle to keep the weight distributed evenly. The sun reflected on the water’s brown surface and warmed his face while the current rocked them. The motion was relaxing, the sort of soft grace that made him forget they were going to snatch snakes out of the woods. From the mountains came the mocking cry of catbirds and crows. Zachary knew that when their song stopped they would be close. Already nothing moved in the high brush.

“Not too far downstream,” Fenton told him.

Not too far turned out to be fifteen more minutes downriver, past the gutted corpse of a Chevy left to house weeds that grew through its open floorboards. Fenton beached them on a small sandbar and the pair climbed out with their sticks.

“Gotta be careful through here,” Fenton said. “Growers about.”

Zachary heard rumors of the marijuana farmers who left fishhooks hanging from trees at eye level, cut out deadfall pits with sharpened sticks like in traps the Vietcong used in the stories old men told at the VFW, but he knew all that talk was horseshit. Rumors served better than real traps. They ascended the hill to silence aside from Fenton’s pole combing through the weeds. Zachary was mindful of his footing. Snakes would likely be sunning in plain sight on the rocks. His mind went back to Mrs. Crawford and the way his father tried to hide her hands in those white gloves. Fear began to make his chest tighten, but something underneath the fear made his skin tingle. It was the same feeling as when he watched the preacher dancing with the snake. He remembered his father's words about fear. If the Lord had given fear to them for a reason, why did he have this other energy surging inside him?

After twenty minutes of beating the brush, Fenton cried out. He stood by a flat hunk of sandstone that must have slid off the mountain, and pointed inside a small crevice. Zachary watched him try to slide the hooked end of his pole underneath. "Giant bastard slid under here."

"Dig him out," Zachary said.

"I can't get under the rock. I need something to wedge it back."

"Then he's gone."

Fear began to make his chest tighten, but something underneath the fear made his skin tingle.

"Come pull it back some," Fenton said. "You get it cleared a few inches and I'll snatch the bastard."

"I ain't getting bit."

"Just use the pole. Don't bitch out."

Zachary bent and slid the metal deep underneath, felt it bite into some unseen part of the rock and began to try and wedge it back. He pulled hard, but it barely shifted. From underneath came the anxious shake of a rattle. He strained until the muscles in his back began to spasm, his hands gone slick with sweat against the pole, but the stone finally began to rise and let the sun light creep in.

"Goddamn," Fenton said. The rock was pulled away enough for Zachary to see a massive writhing coil, a whole legion knotted together until they appeared one massive serpent, heads cocking back to strike. Fenton hooked the wad and hefted it out. Several snakes swam on the end as he danced away. Others fell between his feet and slithered into the grass. The heads moved in a variety of directions, the confused snakes striking at each other in their panic. The rattling continued like a choir singing the same hateful note.

"Get the bag."

Zachary dropped the rock and ran forward with the sack yawning open.

"Hold her open."

The adrenaline was still pounding through him, but watching the snakes snap and twist made the animal hardwiring of fear began to bleed in again, reminding him of how many serpents he'd just ran towards. Still, he was transfixed by the sleek movements on the end of Fenton's pole, the slit eyes meeting his while their forked tongues darted in and out.

"They'll bite me."

"They're too scared to strike."

Zachary didn't know if he believed this, but he held the bag at arm's length while Fenton dumped them inside. Their weight was instant and he nearly dropped the sack before he could tie it shut.

"I think we got enough," he said.

■ ■ ■

Once they were back on the current, Zachary kept bothering the bag. He lifted and gave it a little shake, ran his fingertips over the outside and shifted it from left to right hand, watching the indentations the snakes made as their bodies pushed against the fabric. Fenton motioned for him to put it down, but he went on playing, too pleased to have conquered nature.

"How much you think these are worth?" Zachary asked. "They ain't copperheads."

"Crawford doesn't care for copperheads like he does the ones that sing."

Zachary sat back against the square bow and let his hands dip over the side. It was comforting to feel his fingers drag through the water as the current picked up speed, moving them further downstream away from the funeral home. He brought the cup of his palm up filled with water.

"Sometimes when I'm on these snake runs I like to pretend," Fenton said.

It was an odd admission. Zachary knew they were both too old to pretend, and even though he did it himself from time to time, liked to imagine himself a secret agent in his black suit before he went out to meet the mourners, it wasn't something boys their age weren't meant to tell one another.

"Pretend what?" Zachary asked.

"Pirate, steamboat captain, river raider. Hell, anything but country trash in a stolen truck top."

The creek widened and went wild just ahead. The water broke in white torrents over the few rocks that weren't fully submerged. In the deep pool just past the small rapid sat a Maytag dryer lost during the highest swell of a summer flood. Its front door swung open from a busted hinge.

"Can she make it over those?" Zachary asked.

"Just watch the snakes."

"What about that dryer?"

"If we push hard left we can clear it without tipping over. Just don't let us go into the rocks sideways."

Fenton began using his snake pole to steer. Zachary dipped his pole deep searching for the bottom, but Fenton shook his head.

"Keep it on the snakes."

They hit the rocks hard, their square bow crunching and shaking the raft as it rolled over the white water. Zachary fell back and found his hand on the snake bag. Even through the bag, he could feel their heat in his palm. He let his hand linger imagining the scales against his bare hands, the way Preacher Crawford danced with the serpents in the parking lot. When he looked up, they were turned sideways in the creek and water seeped in from unseen cracks in their hull. Fenton leaned over the front assessing the damage. His pole was missing.

"How bad?" Zachary asked.

"Bent, but not broke. Give me that rod so I can steer."

Zachary handed him the snake rod, but they were already too close to the dryer and still drifting sideways, threatening to collide on their exposed starboard.

Zachary fell back and found his hand on the snake bag. Even through the bag, he could feel their heat in his palm.

"Hold," Fenton said. The water pushed them into the dryer hard enough to lodge it loose from whatever muddy bottom it had settled into. It toppled over, beaching them against it as the truck top split wide and water began to pour in between Zachary's feet, spilling over the lowered side.

"Start swimming," Fenton said.

"What about the snakes?"

Fenton didn't answer. He was already paddling for shore, his arms making long strides as molded shirts from inside the dryer floated by him. The snake bag filled and sank near Zachary. He grabbed it by the string and wrapped it around his arm. The bag's weight and size slowed him, but he managed to dog paddle towards the bank where Fenton already stood hacking up water. The current kept pulling him downstream. He fought hard to keep the shore in sight, focusing on a Gatorade bottle hanging from a bent twig. He would grasp that bottle regardless of how much Cow Creek wanted to drown him.

Something crawled across the ridge of his back, each scale prickling the pimpled skin. The slow rub from the wet body felt rough, the way he imagined a woman's tongue might, as the snake traveled towards his neck. Zachary knew it wanted to coil around his throat, to secure its ride across to the solid sediment of the beach. A part of him wanted to ferry it across, but his mind's eye kept focusing on Mrs. Crawford, on those swelled hands in white gloves. He dove under the water and felt the snake taken from him.

The swim was easier afterwards. Zachary began to beat the current, using it to lead him to the bank where he collapsed in a pile of sumac, panting and staring up at the sky absent a sun. The canopy of the mountains folded in on him and he began to weep as he sputtered out the water he'd swallowed.

Fenton came to stand over him. He'd picked up the discarded bag and began searching for tails to safely untangling the ball of snakes. After tugging at the bodies until he unraveled the massive knot, Fenton lay the drown snakes out in a row like dead soldiers. Zachary rose up and looked over the line as Fenton poked at each one with a stick, prodding them for any sign of life. In the creek, their broken vessel sank.

"Not a single one," Fenton said.

Zachary began to touch each one. He wasn't aware of it, but he was touching them with the same reverence his father touched a body he was about to prepare. He picked up the largest one, a timber rattler thick as his forearm and let the snake dangle the length of his body, the tail in the dirt as he moved the snake's mouth toward his own parted lips. He wanted to hear its rattle come alive, to hear that song of intimidation and death transformed into something else. A sort of music that he knew his ears would never again hear. Fenton spoke, but Zachary was lost in some ritual, his lips kissing the closed mouth of the serpent as he blew his breath into the length of its body. ■

FALLING

Though we are born Clutch-fisted, when we die
We spread our Palmes, and let the world slip by
—William Austin, 1587–1634

He buried his father in March. The preacher preached hellfire—it was that long ago—the creeks were all in flood and the sky had surrendered to the lion. The organ moaned its tinny, electric pulse and the chrysanthemums were cloying and sour. He had hung his head and stepped outside for a cigarette. Although he didn't really laugh, the sky did suddenly empty its rain and the wind pull up its skirts and run free, rising into roaring. And far to the west, the black surf of storm stumbled, and a blue seam of horizon lit with pink and yellow, spread itself above the tree line. He said it might have been God saving himself. It was March. Miracles could be expected. Some years found Easter as well as Good Friday inside its ragged arms. He went walking. Found himself on a swinging bridge staring at the heaving hump of the stream where it divided around rocks still glazed with winter. He told this story only once, how he got in a lot of trouble—leaving the funeral like he did.

Standing on that bridge, watching that sky, ... said he'd never forget the feeling that rose in his throat, the relief when he remembered to breathe again. He'd kept his cards close, the tremble in his hands clutched in the ball of his fists. Still, he'd loved; no one doubted. Call March a sacred month for its contradictions, for its truths. Hard rain. Mud slides. Flood.

And then the night breaks clear, the moon swims in curdled milk, sleep tugs at the stubborn heart. Into his arms he'd remembered falling, opening his eyes, opening his fists.

MARC HARSHMAN

SLING SHOT

Chalk dust. Is returning really so simple? From the hallway, he can see through the open door of the abandoned classroom, through its far window, and out into the hay fields that lay beyond. There is a single bale rotting against the fence. They would stack them, he remembered, build forts from them. The clock, watched so vigilantly, was invisible for the precious minutes of recess. Then the clenched mind relaxed. He need only think where best to set the next bale.

There had been a splinter once, a fine needle of straw under his nail. He had gone to the nurse's office, really just a corner nook behind the big boiler where an old sink stood and a little, mirrored cabinet. She had wonderful, pointy breasts. Never had he fought so hard to keep from crying as when she poured the Mercurochrome onto his bleeding fingertip. She smelled like flowers. Mrs. Smith, his teacher, still had a Valentine poster behind her chair and smelled like death. Sometimes the blackboard grew white as frosted pavement under her furious, prodigious, extravagant handwriting.

He did not have to enter. It was all still there. Going on. He kept looking, though. He could see the red-wing blackbird on the rusted line of barb wire. He could hear its sharp whistle, and somewhere, somewhere near, he could hear his voice as it was then, saying *thank you, Nurse.* And she had kissed the back of his hand.

Just a little more chalk dust, and he was sure he could return, back where the future held none of these ubiquitous clocks that now multiplied around him. There had been only one clock then. One had been enough. And with that one he could make his peace. A single stone, a steady wrist, his good eyes. It had been his favorite game at recess. He only lacked the courage.

MARC HARSHMAN

BLACK HOLES

ANGEL SANDS GUNN

My cousin and her husband, both astrophysicists, wear puffy coats and shiny sunglasses. They step out of their SUV, arriving at our house for the weekend. I haven't spent much time with Laura the last twenty years. I only see her at my mom's annual Christmas Eve party.

Laura's seven-year-old daughter fumbles out of the car and clings to her doll. My girls, just slightly older, escort her into the house. After our initial embrace, Laura and her husband Caleb shift on the crumbling pavement. They peer around, unsure where to look.

"That was quite a drive." Caleb claps his hands, breaking the silence. He's talking about the half-mile, steep and treacherous driveway that twists up our mountain, after the sign at the bottom that warns "Steep Grade. No six-axle vehicles." Mark and I know that they're also stunned by what's at the top—a California mid-century modern, on this red clay mountaintop in Virginia.

The house is in a state of disrepair, in the part of renovations that design magazines never talk about—the "during" phase. This elongated stage comes with an army of workers—jackhammering floors, demolishing walls and cabinets. Before we decided to do this, I heard that renovations could be stressful to marriages, but now I can attest to it. Sometimes, it feels like we pounded a sledgehammer against the foundation of our relationship, to see what makes it crack, opening to all that lies buried beneath.

The exterior of the house is mottled—sections of new, unpainted wood, flanked by shiny copper flashing, other parts painted army green, while a few old boards have been stripped down to redwood.

"The front door's broken." I motion them away from the latticed entrance. "The new one's been ordered," I say, like an apology.

Mark slides open the side door, and we step over the kids' discarded boots, into the living room. A wall of windows wrap around the corners, emulating Frank Lloyd Wright. I have read that this era of modern house was built to let the outside in and to reflect the design of nature. However, I feel vulnerable in its wide-open spaces, like a fox stranded from its hole.

We point across the way to the distant ski mountain and to Charlottesville, in the valley below. Mountains circle the town like the crust of a crater.

We offer drinks and ask them about living in D.C. Caleb works for NASA in Huntsville most of the time, but was invited to the Capital for six months.

His team recently discovered solar flares. I searched the phenomenon before their visit. I still don't fully understand, but I imagine it like a cartoon, with solar fire splashing outwards like burning darts, the sun a hungry monster in the sky.

I never took physics. When my biology teacher in high school encouraged me to tackle it, I laughed. I never liked the unforgiving rectitude of equations, didn't understand how there could only be one correct answer. I preferred the ambiguity of language.

Laura is a physicist, too, but her career was interrupted by a bout with breast cancer. She doesn't talk about how she

I have read that this era of modern house was built to let the outside in and to reflect the design of nature. However, I feel vulnerable in open spaces, like a fox stranded from its hole.

nearly died in breast replacement surgery afterwards, but she and Caleb joke about the results.

"This is all me." She giggles, crossing her legs and spreading her hand on the granite. She explains that the doctor used flesh from her belly to replace breast tissue. Her eyes slant upwards, her big laugh bursting out like it did when she was a child. Even though she has outgrown them, I still picture her freckles.

Laura and I grew up together in Memphis. Our moms were sisters. Her mom, single and working, mine stayed home with my brothers and me. Laura often spent her days at our house, before we started school. We were close. Almost like sisters ourselves.

We used to play dress-up with my dance costumes. We twirled on the green shag carpet next to the tube stereo. Laura made silly faces stretching her thin white arms, mocking ballet, making my pink tutu bounce. I laughed and leapt in red sequins, raising brown arms to circle my head.

Laura never wanted to leave our little yellow house on Ivanhoe Cove. She would hide the moment her mother's car pulled onto the bumpy drive. Sometimes, it took an hour before her mother found her and dragged her from our front foyer.

Laura lived across town in a rental house, and when I went to play there, she never wanted our time together to end. She would chase our car down the road, waving her hands wildly, until her spindly legs couldn't keep up any more.

One time at her house—we must have been six or seven—we were kicking dirt in her backyard, between the cyclone fence and Wolf River bottoms. The cool air smelled like mud. Electric lines hung messily above us, over brown grass. She pointed to the moon, which was faded and pocked in the daylight. I told her I didn't understand how the moon and sun could both be out at the same time. I thought they were the same thing, rising orange in day, fading white at night. She was younger, but already understood the world better. She elbowed me.

"How can you not know that?"

■ ■ ■

Back in the kitchen, Mark and Caleb slip out through the glass door to the patio. They carry lighters and flashlights for the grill. Laura and I check the girls. In the hallway, we hear them playing in the bedroom. We sneak away from their door, and I lead Laura to my office, the little room behind the kitchen, though nobody but me would call it that.

I have been compiling stories about my grandmother who died in May. She was Laura's grandmother, too—our mothers' mother. I wasn't close to her. I think she loved me. She placed her hand on her heart, on the other side of her Macy's nametag, every time I came to town and visited her. She mentioned cards I sent, stories my mom told her about my life. But she was always inaccessible. For various reasons, I guess—her alcoholic son, her late holiday hours, the indescribable affliction of not being able to have close relationships. She only made rare appearances at family gatherings and usually avoided them altogether. Laura was the only one of the grandchildren who got to spend time with her. Mimi sometimes babysat Laura when she was young—when Laura wasn't with me.

I tell Laura how I've been writing a novel based on Mimi's childhood and that I called her a year before she died and interviewed her.

Up until that day, an answering machine vetted her calls, and my uncle, who lived with her, intercepted, never letting anyone get through. This time, though, I emailed him directly and made arrangements. I told him I was writing a book about a family living on a West Virginia mountain in the 1930s. My uncle scheduled a time for my call.

It felt strange to hear my grandmother's voice on the phone, still sharp and elegant, trilling lightly over consonants, telling stories from eighty-five years before, memories sharp as diamonds.

"I never even heard about the Depression. Never knew about it. We were totally self-sufficient. It was a large farm. With two big gardens. Fields of corn and beans. We grew everything—lettuce, carrots, watermelons, squash, sweet potatoes, peanuts—in winter we'd roast them and throw shells in the fireplace. Some days, we'd load up the truck with Dad and take food to the coal mines. We'd ask him, are these people poor? 'No, we just have more than we need.'"

I read our grandmother's words to Laura, thinking she knows the stories. My mother has told me stories about Mimi my whole life, but Laura shakes her head.

"I never knew any of this."

I read more, still hearing my grandmother's crisp lilt in my ears, still able to picture her startling blue eyes, her expressive hands folded officially in her lap, her nails shaped and polished frosty pink. I can almost smell the Pond's cold cream she used on her face, remember the touch of her gold pin stuck sharply through her lapel, smell the Aquanet on her thick, teased hair.

"My first boyfriend, Norman Mills. We met at church. He came home with me and had dinner. Mama was glad. If we hadn't married by sixteen, she said 'People are going to talk.'" My grandmother laughed. "She would've wanted me to marry at thirteen!"

I tell Laura that Mimi attended Mountain Baptist Church when she was a girl.

"They would preach and try and scare you half to death. What they didn't scare us with, mother would. Hellfire and brimstone. When you died, the devil came, got the pitchfork and threw you in the fire, and you would burn forever and ever. I didn't believe it. I would go out in the woods and get up on the stump and dare The Lord to strike me dead this minute, and I knew it didn't work. I always had to prove things to myself. If somebody tried to scare me, it just worked the other way."

"She was so strong." Laura bites her thumb, her eyes shining. She doesn't seem to know about Mimi's affairs, the several times my grandmother persuaded my grandfather to move cross-country, only to take up with another man, or to write clandestine letters to her sister's husband. I know Laura is aware that our grandmother abandoned her children when they were young, and I assume that she knows how Mimi climbed out the bathroom window, leaving a note behind.

"You'll be better off without me."

Laura shakes her head, never having heard the line. She wants to hear more, but the girls have come into my office. They are a coalition.

"We want a snack."

I hear the glass doors slide open.

I can almost smell the Pond's cold cream she used on her face, remember the touch of her gold pin stuck sharply through her lapel, smell the Aquanet on her thick, teased hair.

"Where are the tongs?" Mark bellows through the open back door.

I select "Save," then click the red dot before closing the lid of my computer. Laura begs for more.

"I'll send it to you."

She grabs my hand. We stop and press our hands together. We have forgotten. They are the same size. Our fingers push together, a perfect match.

■ ■ ■

We sit at the long oak table in the living room. Laura helps Emily, cutting her meat, telling her to remove her elbows from the table. Sally, my youngest, licks butter from her bread, and her sister Grace looks around the table for a cue, whether to wait for prayer or to eat without one. It feels nice to have our families gathered. Darkness through the windows now conceals us, making the room cozier. Candles cast a yellow light. A fire burns behind glass.

Mark cuts the crisp, brown flesh from the bone and divides onto the remaining plates. He loves to obsess over the perfect juicy texture, experimenting with cuts, his current favorite the giant Tomahawk steak. It looks like something cavemen ate, a comic bulk of flesh surrounding a handle-like bone, something to play tennis with, or to scare away wild animals. Red juice pools on my plate.

There is fidgeting and silence at the table as we begin to eat. I quickly summon my mother—she always knows how to make dinner conversation ignite, asking guests about their professions or travels. By inviting them to share, she puts them at ease, and words flow like wine.

"Girls, do you know that Caleb is a scientist who studies space?"

They nod, looking interested, and I ask Caleb to tell us something. He chews his steak and glances towards the redwood ceiling.

"Do you know about black holes?"

I think bottomless pits, time vacuums, fictional vortexes to other universes.

"Black holes exist. In our galaxy. We're tracking them right now."

We are all fascinated. The girls ask questions. Caleb draws diagrams in the air. He tells us about a star called S2 that orbits a region called Sagittarius A. I didn't even know that black holes were real. I laugh to myself at my lack of scientific knowledge. I am like people who thought the world was flat, persisting in ignorance, drawing incorrect conclusions about their lives.

Later that night, while the girls retreat to my bedroom to watch TV, the adults sit on the low brown sofa in front of the fire. Mark and Caleb laugh over a bottle of Scotch and swirl their glasses. Laura asks me to tell her more about what Mimi said. We lean forward clutching glasses of red wine. A floor lamp casts yellow light in a small pool around us.

Laura went to Memphis last spring, too, when our grandmother was dying. She drove up from Huntsville for the day, and I flew down for the week. We hugged at Mimi's bedside, a rare second visit in a year.

I wanted to be there for my mom. In Mimi's final decade, my mom learned to forgive her mother for her absences. After twenty years of living with another man, Mimi had returned to my grandfather. She had nowhere to turn, and my grandfather with great generosity welcomed her, glad for her company, after the years alone. However, coming back didn't mean she was going to be a wife, or a mother, for that matter. She still held the family at a distance, but, in the end, my mom accepted whatever her mother could give. She learned not to expect more. She seemed satisfied to visit her mother at work and help whenever her mother allowed.

I was pleased by my mother's forgiveness. She was happier, and I enjoyed hearing the stories. How Mimi won sales prizes at work, the funny things she said, the time she stopped thieves at Macy's, the time a homeless man approached her on the sidewalk.

"Give me your purse," he said. But Mimi was quick, not missing a beat.

"I'm homeless, too." She clutched the handle of her grocery cart, a dark raincoat covering her work clothes. She looked him in the eyes.

"I'm sorry, ma'am." The man replied and shuffled away.

The part that I couldn't align was that Mimi never apologized. Never even acknowledged the fact that she left. I thought that might happen on her deathbed and wanted to be there when it did.

■ ■ ■

Back in my living room, I grasp the leather chair, not sure how much Laura knows about our grandmother's death. I ask her if she knew that Mimi refused pain medicine, while in hospice. Laura squints her eyes.

"My mom never tells me anything."

I wonder what to say. Maybe her mom doesn't want her to know. Maybe my mom doesn't want me to share the stories. Are they secrets?

"Did your mom tell you what Uncle Andy said?" I think of his half-deranged confession, that his birth certificate "has two things on it that nobody knows." He held wobbly fingers in the air, still shaky from years of intoxication, even though he was now sober.

The part that I couldn't align was that Mimi never apologized. Never even acknowledged the fact that she left.

Mark adds more hickory to the fire. We pour another glass of wine. A drip streaks the stem of the glass dark red. I struggle to put it in order, what to say first. I think of how Mimi never saw a doctor for the cancer eating her colon from the inside. Despite her pain, she kept going to work, without complaint. She stood on the white marble floor of the men's department while blood poured from her body and soaked through her feminine pad. My mother watched from behind a rack of clothes while Mimi smiled at customers, folding men's Levi's, directing them to the rack of Ralph Lauren dress shirts. My mom waited for her mother to be alone. But when the customer left, my mom saw Mimi lean against the counter, hang her head and close her eyes, refueling for the fight.

"Mother, are you okay?" My mom put her hand on Mimi's blazer.

Mimi jumped, then recomposed herself.

"Just taking a break." She told my mom not to worry. "I'll be fine."

It turned out she was already sick and knew it would be fatal, but she powered on.

Instead, I tell Laura about my visit, how Mimi refused morphine.

"She never had taken any medicine, except once—antibiotics for an earache."

The other thing I tell Laura is Mimi's favorite church songs—"The Old Rugged Cross" and "Shall We Gather at the River." I don't know them, but Laura played piano at church throughout her childhood and nods, calculating an invisible melody in her head. She walks directly to our piano, pushes the pedals and plants her hands, open-fingered across the ivory keys. We all look up from our glasses and watch as music rises like a ghost. Filling the room with the sounds of another time and place.

■ ■ ■

Later that weekend, after my cousin's family leaves, I look up black holes. I notice an essay by Stephen Hawking with a down-to-earth title, "Does God Play Dice?"

I learn that Hawking recently made a discovery that black holes "ain't so black." Hawking illustrates in his colloquial manner, and I can actually follow the explanation. He says that once matter goes into a black hole, some particles get transmitted as light, while the hole itself eventually disappears. He concludes that, "What all this means is, that information will be lost from our region of the universe, when black holes are formed, and then evaporate. This loss of information will mean that we can predict even less than we thought." Black holes aren't just hiding matter, as previously conjectured. They deconstruct and erase matter. Forever. Hawking says that this discovery stands science on its head and concludes, "The universe does not behave according to our pre-conceived ideas. It continues to surprise us."

■ ■ ■

The next morning, everybody but me goes back to work and school, leaving me alone in a quiet house. It is an unseasonable winter day, with forecasts of almost sixty degrees. The mountains shine green under the vast blue sky, and it seems I have an aerial view of Earth, as you picture it from space, blue and green swirled together like a yin-yang sign.

I carry tea to my office and settle down to find the notes for Laura. I open the file on my computer and remember sitting with my mom and aunt at my grandmother's bedside, during the last week of her life. We were trying to distract her from her pain as she lay there, still beautiful, even more beautiful. The wash-in-dye faded from her steel grey waves. Her thick make-up washed away, revealing lucid, dewy skin, set off by crystalline blue eyes. She lay beside us, but at a distance, grappling with her own pain. At moments, she seized up, gripping her fist, wincing her face. Then, she'd relax and smile, noticing us, as if saying, "Are you still here?"

In the lulls, she returned to reverie.

"Mother, what are you thinking about?" My mom leaned in so Mimi could hear. My grandmother played with the corner of her sheets.

I pressed the button on my phone to record, to remember her exact words.

"Seven sisters would walk five miles to school and five miles back. When it rained the branches would lean over, and we couldn't make it, so we'd stop in to see a neighbor who lived on the Little Bluestone River. She didn't have any children, and we really looked forward to spending the day with her when we couldn't get to school. The couple had never been able to have children, and they asked my parents for one of their children. Because they had seven, and the couple didn't have any."

My grandmother's parents said "We wouldn't trade any of our children for a million dollars." Mimi, prostrate in her bed, looked solemn, but her lip curled.

"I just prayed they would take me."

■ ■ ■

On the night when the pain became unbearable, Mimi finally started morphine. She rang the bell several times, but my uncle didn't come. She dreamt of "bad men with swords." Still confused, she whimpered, "I hope they don't have their scythes when they come back." She thought they were going to "stick them right through her." She said she thought "robbers" had come into her house and tied up her son. Then, she told me that it was the neighbors who had all come and were having a "pig on a poke" in the driveway, roasting a whole hog. The neighbors turned to her and jeered.

"You've been porked."

It sounded gruesome, as she described the scene. The neighbors had little bags with tags on them that said "You've been pigged" and "You've been porked," and they left all their trash, all their "pig stuff" in her driveway.

After she retold the nightmare, the medicine started working, and she settled down. My mom and I tried to soothe her. My mom asked her what she was thinking and she again recollected. She recited a nursery rhyme, "Little Bo Peep has lost her sheep and doesn't know where to find them…" and told us how she always loved animals.

On the last day of my visit, I sat next to my mom and aunt, crowded together beside her bed, sharing a chair between us. Mimi was still coherent, though subdued with the right dose of morphine. There had been no more nightmares.

She turned to look in our faces, her blue eyes now placid. She smiled, and I thought perhaps it was the moment we all were waiting for.

"If I had it all to do again," Mimi sustained a gesture, as if lifting a precious gem in the cup of her hand. Her eyes twinkled. The three of us held our breaths, hoping for repentance or apology.

"I'd be my same old sneaky self." She closed her eyes, and we sighed. Then, we looked at each other and couldn't suppress our laughter, amazed at this proud, mysterious woman.

■ ■ ■

After my trip to Memphis, Mark and I see a double rainbow as we drive into Charlottesville on our way to a restaurant. I tell him it is a sign. He reaches across the car. His pulse beats in his palm, in time with mine, like we are one beating heart. A few minutes later, my cell phone rings with confirmation from my mother. Mimi has died.

I think how Laura would laugh if she read that. Surely, the symbolic meaning of rainbows has no grounding in science, yet I cling to the belief, to the hope they offer.

Maybe I shouldn't mail Laura these transcripts and unearth the stories that died with Mimi. In her absence, perhaps, the family only wants to remember the pleasant parts—the good times together, the funny stories, Mimi's beautiful face. Maybe the truth will be too painful, resurrecting the suffering everyone wants to leave behind. I think about the black holes Caleb and Stephen Hawkings described. Maybe I should stop digging, stop trying to crack down beneath the foundation of everything. And let the past go—like matter in a black hole—so it's wiped out forever, and the rainbow is all that remains. ■

MOLLY IN A RED WIG PLAYS A FIDDLE

Molly asks me take the hanging guitar
held suspended from its two-prong hook screwed
to the wall. The guitar is her brother's,
custom-made in Viet Nam, a body
brown as roux, its head and neck completely
filigreed with inlayed nacre. Hank is
working as a lawyer in Saigon. At first, I
close my eyes and let my searching fingers
find the old positions as in rhythm
I start strumming one four five. She never
names the tunes she plays, just calls them "old ones,"
Gaelic melodies through Appalachian
ache discovered by a West Coast woman
travelled more than I will ever travel.
"Do you know some Hank?" she asks me. *Which ol'*
Hank, I think, *your brother whose guitar I'm*
chording now or everybody's Hank? I
smile and nod; I wonder which of them she'll
draw, "I Saw the Light," "Your Cheatin' Heart"? No,
neither one will fit tonight. She settles
on a plaintive "I'm So Lonesome, I Could
Cry," and I am watching Molly's bow; she
never counts, her timing shifts for feeling,
she keeps playing 'til imagined dancers
drop, and neither of us knows the lyrics
front to back; they're just familiar lonesome
lines the other guests forgot the words to,
first duet, too blue, October evening.

THOMAS ALAN HOLMES

SEVENTY-TWO DEGREE
MID-FEBRUARY DAY

A lone honey bee wanders the air
yawning some stiff memory of flight
abruptly awake and called out of safety
to duty by a whisper understood only
as an ancient vibration of color and taste
methodical over mostly absent green
landscape bloomless but for plastic flowers
marking other still hibernating things

The crocuses sound confused
with their little preemptive voices
of purple and yellow and white
too early Easter eggs perhaps
winking up to light's surprise
the clouds now darkening with coolness
but laced of Saffron and offering
only the scent of a final mission

I swear I can smell things
under the ground sometimes
heavy dirt hints at where the irises
and spearmint are spreading
where the crocuses are strolling
are these as dormant as we suspect
or do they keep vigil with the most
diligent bees who dare to roam in winter?

LARRY THACKER

JUDE

AMY CLARK

The only thing of mine to survive the fire was a picture of Holly Hobbie Mommy made before Jude was born, her belly swollen as she stood in her sister's kitchen. Her hair was cut in a shag like Jane Fonda's in the picture on the Frigidaire, but frosted. Her long-sleeved oxford shirt, a man's going-to-church-shirt, hung to the hem of a pair of cutoff jean shorts. She and my aunt Leigh were barefoot, their toes bright red jewels half-buried in the brown shag carpet.

I can still smell the sweet smoke curling above emerald ashtrays near the kitchen sink where they dipped pictures in water before lifting them to drip. When I held the ash tray to the sun, it glowed through the bubbles forever frozen in glass. My aunt Leigh brought the joint to her lips, squinting, before she passed it to Mommy. Abba sang from the dark wood of the stereo cabinet in the corner of the living room, their words drifting, sailing in the hazy air. I tried to eavesdrop on Mommy and Leigh talking in the softest parts of the songs.

"Drunk again?" That's Leigh. "How many times does that make this week?"

Mommy lifted the picture of Holly Hobbie from a pan of water, held it until the drips slowed.

"I don't know. I don't keep count."

Leigh scrubbed a piece of cedar with steel wool. She rinsed it and handed it to Mommy, who draped Holly Hobbie over the face of the wood and centered it. Leigh picked up the joint and toked again, exhaled with a long sigh. "You can move in with me. Bill won't care a bit."

My first memory of Bill, my aunt's boyfriend, is holding his hand as I balanced on new, plastic roller skates at the playground near Leigh's trailer park where she lived for a while after she moved out of the apartment. She did not live there long, because Bill was "self-made," she always told me, "in the money." He had inherited his dad's tire business, then bought a funeral home. The same funeral home where daddy's body would be laid in a closed casket, Jude in his arms. A year later, it would be filled to the ceiling with rank river water in the flood of '77, which pulled caskets from the ground and carried them downstream along with mattresses, insulation, milk crates, dead animals. The water would fill up the first floor of

Leigh's apartment building, climb the stairs to the foot of her door, but no further. When the waters came down, they would find caskets lodged in the arms of trees.

But in this memory Daddy is still alive and Jude would be born that summer. The smells in Leigh's apartment stayed with me for the next thirty years like a security blanket. Years later, I would seek them out, hover near them like a moth. I would sit in beauty salons, pretending to read a magazine as I'm inhaling, drowning in my past. I'd smoke pot because that smell is the closest I can get to her.

Mommy laughed. It was her polite laugh, short and subtle, not her genuine laugh that bubbled up from the belly. A macramé owl hanger with two big eyes blocked part of her face from my view. It held a potted vine that fell gracefully to the floor where it had begun to coil. She stroked the picture with a sponge, erasing the bubbles and imperfections until the surface was smooth.

"If this one's a boy," Mommy said, "he'll be a fool for it."

Holly Hobbie hung in my room, framed in the glow of the security light where bats swooped and dived for bugs. She stood in profile, holding wildflowers, her face hidden by her enormous bonnet. Her head was bowed as if she were praying-or maybe crying—like she knew what was to come.

■ ■ ■

The night Jude was born I waited with my Granny Bobbie, Daddy's mother, who smoked Vantage while we watched *The Grinch Who Stole Christmas* on her rabbit-eared set. I sat on blankets spread on the floor eating cheese crackers. Granny Bobbie had a red lava lamp, light shining through star-shaped holes in its base. We were bathed in the blue of the television set, perched on its cart with wheels, and surrounded by the amber glow of lava bubbles the color of blood as they merged and split. I was mesmerized, casting my gaze between the oozing, red lava and the greenish Grinch. That was as close as Granny Bobbie got to a Christmas tree.

The aqua blue telephone next to her chair rang after I had fallen asleep on the floor, and it jarred me awake. Bobbie had covered me with one of her afghans, loosely crocheted in variegated yarn in several shades of brown and cream. Nearly everything in her house was brown, except the phone and the lava lamp.

"Does he have a head full of hair?" she said, pulling on her cigarette. I could hear my dad's voice in murmurs. Bobbie chuckled. "Hit won't stay that color. Ava do alright?" Daddy's voice again. I heard a high "Yeah," then his deep voice fell on a sigh. I imagined him with the pay phone to his ear, strands of hair falling below a baseball cap, two fingers on his skinny hip holding a cigarette.

We were bathed in the blue of the television set, perched on its cart with wheels, and surrounded by the amber glow of lava bubbles the color of blood as they merged and split.

The lava curled and oozed through a veil of smoke, and I drifted back toward sleep as Bobbie put the phone back on the cradle, settling with a clack. Through heavy-lidded eyes I gazed at the lamp. I'd once seen a picture on PBS of lava shooting from a volcano. I asked Daddy why it was red. "Hot as a thousand suns," Daddy said. "Burns everything in its path."

"Be a good girl," Bobbie said in a voice full of gravel, "and you can have that lamp when I'm dead." In our mountain tongue, the vowels in lamp sounded like those in rain. I don't know if I made her nervous, or if she was a kidder, but Bobbie promised I could have something when she died, every time I came to her house. I figured by the time it happened I'd be rich. I once found a bracelet in the bathroom near an ornate liquor bottle where she kept her mouthwash. I carried the bracelet to her, wordless, presented it as if to ask if this, too, could go on the death-gift wish list. She looked up from the book she was reading, *Dallas*, and she nodded. The cigarette between her lips bobbed as she said, "When I'm dead."

I still think back on that offer, wondering if she felt badly for me since the baby meant I'd be getting less attention, wondering if it was her way of softening the blow. But I never felt jealous of Jude, not that I can remember.

She would see her son and grandson buried four months from that night, but she wouldn't follow them to the grave for twenty-two more years. I wonder, when the telephone rang on the day they died, whether she imagined it was my jealousy that fed the fire, or the awkward fumblings of a six year-old who only wanted to throw a paper towel into the woodstove like the grown-ups.

■ ■ ■

I see Jude in a dream, every now and then, but he's old enough to be walking, as if he's grown in death. When I was six, Jude was just months into his life, sleeping in the back bedroom between two pillows on a purple chintz bedspread, his fist tucked near his neck. I'd watch him nap, study his little crabapple chin move as if he were trying to talk in his sleep, his eyelashes a series of commas against his cheeks.

Daddy was sleeping, too, his body too long for the couch. Daddy was long all over, long neck, long nose, long fingers, long feet that hung over the bed or propped on the arm of the couch, like a V. "It's the Carter build," Granny Bobbie would say. "Your boy'll be a picker or a baseball player." I remember Daddy's arm hooked over his head, both hands curled into fists like his baby son's, the one he wanted so bad but not bad enough to stop his drinking, which is why he was asleep at four o'clock in the afternoon.

I was always the last off the bus, no matter how fast Terry, the driver, hooked it around the curves in our holler. He had grown up there, too, Terry and all seven of his brothers and sisters. They had gone to school with Daddy, so he knew how fast he could go, knew every dip and washboard on that dirt road. I think about Terry sometimes, and wonder if he pretended he was the pilot he'd always wanted to be, a sky jockey, soaring as if the rises and dips in our road were clouds, pockets of air that made it rumble. My school was only four miles away but his route took us clear to the border of the next county and back through a maze of winding roads until the bus coughed me up at the end of the driveway in a cloud of dust.

It was my first year of school. Kindergarten.

Mommy took off work on my first day so she could be there when I got off the bus, one of my last memories of her. She and Leigh sat in lawn chairs in the front yard, breaking green beans and drinking Tab. Just beyond their lawn chairs there was a garden, and just beyond that, a tobacco field where the stalks had grown taller than Daddy. Somebody else would have to sucker, cure, grade, and sell our tobacco that year. Strange, the things my mind holds onto, like pieces of thread, like stray mints at the bottom of a purse. I remember Mommy's tank top, how the straps had shifted, the white lines of her skin cutting through the sunburn that crept across her collarbone and shoulders on one side. She always smelled like baby oil. Baby oil and Tab. She wasn't home the day Jude and Daddy died. I was. But I was only six. That's what people have said to me over the years. Leigh and Bill, therapists, boyfriends. You were only six, as if being older would have made me more accountable, as if I could have grabbed Daddy by those long feet and dragged him off the couch and down the porch steps, or carried Jude like the baby doll I pretended he was and placed him safely in the grass. Away from the choking smoke that everyone says took his life before the fire reached him.

As if that makes it easier.

But I don't feel traumatized, or carry this heavy guilt, not really. "How do your dreams about Jude make you feel?" All the therapists ask me that. I go to them because of the dreams, mostly, because I want to figure them out.

"Disrupted," I always say. Like a hiccup that I can't get rid of. Seeing Jude is unsettling in an otherwise settled life. When he appears he can be a child, occasionally a teenager, and once he looked as if he were thirty. His eyes are still blue but that dark hair is grown out thick and curly, his arms and legs are long and lean like Daddy's. As a teenager, Jude has a ponytail like one of the guys I was dating when I dreamed of him. Mommy joked when he was born that the dark hair was the Cherokee coming out in him, and Daddy huffed that the Carters were Scots-Irish so he doubted that.

I imagine a sketch artist living in the basement of my subconscious mind, hunched over, hand sweeping a canvas, drawing these pictures of Jude.

"Do you think," one therapist asked-because they always ask, as if I'm the one with all the answers though they are posing their own answers as questions-"Jude appears at the same age you are at the time of the dream?"

And I know what that question means. "Do you feel guilty about being alive at ten, twenty, thirty because Jude could not live to be those ages?"

"Why?" I say. "Because I was the one who burned down the house?"

The chin lowers, the head angles with empathy, eyes look at me over the tops of glasses. You were only six. I anticipate it and my lips move with theirs. "Only six."

At six, my head was big and my arms and legs were Pixie sticks, so birdlike Terry called me Chicken Little. "How's it goin' Chicken Little?" he'd say around the wad of tobacco he kept in his left cheek, one thick hand on the bus door lever. I could barely lift Jude, and I wasn't allowed to try unless Mommy or Daddy was there but I did it once without their permission because I wanted to feel his heft in my arms. I stole into the bedroom where he slept, always in the middle of the bed because he wouldn't sleep in the crib, and I slid my tiny forearms beneath twelve pounds of him and felt him roll toward me. What I remember is how warm he was and how much heavier than I expected. I tried to shift him onto my shoulder the way Mommy carried him but the blanket fell away and then tangled itself around my arm and I struggled under his weight, his head dangling to one side, then backward.

I stole into the bedroom where he slept, always in the middle of the bed because he wouldn't sleep in the crib, and I slid my tiny forearms beneath twelve pounds of him...

"What are you doing?" I heard Mommy in the bedroom doorway. She sounded amused, not at all angry. I froze, clinging to a still-sleeping Jude and waiting for her to rescue him from whatever grown-up thing I'd been trying to do with my six year-old pixie arms.

The truth is this, and eventually we always get to it because all therapy comes down to one's relationship with one's mother, is that not true? The truth is that as disruptive as my dreams about Jude are, I am more bothered by other things.

■ ■ ■

I sat between Uncle Bill and Aunt Leigh at the funeral, as if they had already adopted me, as if they knew Mommy would not recover from the state she was in the way she walked aimlessly from room to room at night like she was searching for Jude. The way her eyes stared, glassy, at his casket when I tried to talk to her. "It's the drugs they give her," I heard somebody behind us say.

The casket was silver, covered in white roses. I think back on that now and wonder if white was a deliberate choice. Anything but the color of fire. Of embers.

The funeral home was small, paneled in dark wood and lit by fluorescent lights that buzzed over our heads. Thin, green carpet covered floors that creaked. The casket was flanked by a cross made of flowers on one side and a wreath made of flowers on the other, a lamb nestled in its center.

Leigh didn't set me beside Mommy. She sat beside her, one arm around her shoulders, the other holding her hand. Mommy kept her eyes fixed on her lap during the organ music, during the obituary reading, during prayer. A tissue was balled in her fist. I remember that my feet did not reach the floor and so I swung them back and forth. I heard weeping throughout the room, a cough. I felt stares press the back of my head, and I wished for it all to be over.

A preacher took the podium, his Bible in hand, dark hair greased and combed to one side. He began to read and talk, and at some point during his sermon his voice rose and

Mommy began to rock back and forth. Leigh tightened her arm around her shoulders and murmured in her ear. Granny Bobbie, who sat on the other side of Mommy, put her arm around her, too.

The preacher's shouting hurt my ears. I tugged on Bill's jacket and told him I needed to pee. He took my hand and we walked toward a door that slid into the wall. A man in a suit opened it for us. The floor groaned with every step, and a thousand eyes seemed to follow us. I heard a loud moan behind me.

I used the bathroom and then waited while Bill went outside to smoke. I looked up at a picture of Jesus with his soft wavy hair, high cheekbones and long, thin, gently bearded face, his eyes tender and gazing upward. When I moved to the right or to the left, Jesus' face melted into another image: his emaciated body hanging on a cross in the midst of a storm. If I stepped one way or the other, lightning zig-zagged in the sky above the cross. I shuffled to the left and back to the right in a little dance, the floor covered in thin, pea-green carpet protesting under my feet, my stare fixated on the hologram where the cross with Jesus' dead body morphed into his alive, kind face and back again. How awful, to see the face of a man with such tender, hopeful eyes followed by his murdered body, hanging in a most undignified way, not surrounded by flowers and organ music and loving family. Inside the room where the doors slid into the brown, paneled walls, the preacher hollered, his voice piercing the air. I was used to preachers yelling about what had been done to this man. But the hologram gave me a whole new perspective.

Later on, in a new bed in Leigh and Bill's house with a bedspread printed in tiny rainbows, I'd dream about the picture at the funeral home, too. But in this dream, when I step to the right or left, Jesus' face becomes Jude's. Jude at thirty-something, gazing at me in sorrow, because he has to die so many times. ■

BLUE TICK MONGREL,
PACING THE PITTSYLVANIA COUNTY LINE

This blacktop tells of possum scent
But I lead myself to a red dirt rising,
Where lanky pine trees bend
And whistle in wind.
I stop and sniff, then pace
Again, a dog intent on going somewhere.

I travel with squared haunches
Past tobacco fields all yellow
With a tawny scent and let
The bumblebee buzz me by.
Even in sleep my paws twitch
With the dream of this plateau:
I'm running to the creaking pines,
Orange with dust, padding over silent straw.

Let me be I tell the truck:
I left my shaded yard months ago.
Strange men with smokehouses
Shall not capture me though at night I bay
For hearths and table scraps I've forsaken.

I am the hound you find pacing, up
Into the curve of scarlet horizons.
My blood tells in the way I hang my head
And move a little side-ways
That I have a coyote way of knowing—

Somewhere close there's a circle
Of raccoon eyes, high
Among pines that praise the sky.

ANNIE WOODFORD

LANDFALL

ERICA LANGSTON

I am thirteen, standing in front of the full-length mirror in the bathroom, naked. Florida summer heat presses hard against the house, seeping in through thin walls. It's hurricane season. The window unit chugs and sputters in an attempt to trim thick waves of heat into wisps of cool relief. It's failing. The air is stagnant. My hands and armpits are clammed with sweat. My body is ashen and blurred against the sickly pink walls reflecting in the mirror. The shower drips uninterrupted.

Baby fat clings to large curves that should be sharply defined by now. Other areas are overdeveloped, underdeveloped, misshaped, and awkward. I wonder how this would be divided on a butcher's chart. Dense shoulders, a rigid square chest with two banana-boobs splayed in opposite directions, a deep belly button, all rest on two giant loaves of raw dough. Parts that were once taught move and jiggle. Things are not so uniform any more. I dry off, put on my clothes, and make my way to the backyard where my mother is waiting with splintered wood and rusty screws. A storm is coming.

My mother is crouched at the foot of an unbalanced ladder. The dirt is littered with a fresh deposit of her morning cigarette butts. Puffed pouches of sleeplessness rest loosely under her eyes. A storm is pressing down on the Bahamas, clearing a path to the tip of South Florida. It's due to make landfall tomorrow evening. We have ten windows to board-up. We aren't speaking. The yard smells of decay. Garbage overflows from crinkled aluminum drums resting against the side of the house. Piles of dry white dog shit and abandoned Tonka trucks interrupt the flat earth. Lost marbles cling to lips of dirt and reflect the midday sun like stars in a night sky. I pick up a board of plywood. Its edges, sharp and uneven, cut into my palms. My grip is weak. I press it against the sun-bleached stucco and wait for my mother to drill last season's screws into the wood. We do this for four hours in silence.

We are interrupted by the babies. They roll through the yard like tumbleweeds, a competing entanglement of arms and legs, kicking and screaming and slapping. My mother stops our work to separate the babies and disappears into the house with the youngest one clinging to her leg in tears. The five-year-old, the winner, a girl, picks up the abandoned drill and begins driving it into the dirt. Her curls are matted against the back of her neck in layers of sweat. She is focused, licking at the crust of nose drippings on her upper lip, drilling into the earth beneath her bare feet. A strap of her faded blue tank top droops off her shoulder. “Allie,” I call to her, “Allie, don’t do that.” She ignores me with such deft I wonder if I’ve spoken out loud. I sit on a broken edge of concrete jutting out from beneath the house and watch her. There is a shift in the air, not movement, not wind, just a light ease of pressure as clouds move over the noon sun. “Allie,” I say again. Nothing.

■ ■ ■

“We have to prepare,” a news anchor announces over the store speakers, “for the worst.” The voice echoes through a grid of empty aisles. It’s a hit that dominates the airwaves each August. Every radio station has played it repeatedly for the last four days. It’s the season for panic.

I am fifteen, waiting for my mother to cash a check at the customer service desk. I have the youngest baby resting on one hip and a bag of canned goods digging into the other. Birds flutter and chirp through the rafters. The shelves have been mobbed. The floor is veined with scuffmarks and swirls of weeks-old dust. The produce section yields overpowering ripeness. A box of batteries has been slashed and partially pocketed, leaving half the pack scattered in front of the checkout line. They roll like marbles across the stained linoleum. The air smells of abandon. A bagger pushes a cart of empty crates and kicks the batteries out of his way as he passes.

The woman standing in line in front of my mother eclipses the register with a small gang of toddlers and demands to know how the fuck a grocery store can run out of diapers the day before a hurricane. The cashier picks up the phone and announces that assistance is needed.

I set the canned goods at my mother's feet, readjust the child on my hip, and walk to the front of the store to examine the storm preparedness display that greets a steady flow of desperate shoppers. Three science boards line a card table, creating a mini theatre featuring previous disasters. A red, hard font stamps the unbounded question "Are You Prepared?" across the top of the exhibit. Snapshots Hurricane Andrew remind passersby of the potential this season holds. The photos show a line of men filing around my elementary school gym, holding empty milk jugs and paint buckets, waiting for water rations and packets of macaroni. Uprooted trees wrapped in streamers of sheet metal decorate the streets of downtown. Overturned cars balance atop one another like Jenga pieces.

I untack the picture of the men from the board and examine their faces. They are my uncles, neighbors, father. None of them are looking at the camera. Their eyes are dazed and distant, post-traumatic. There is urgency in their stance. They are deflated, winded, wide-eyed children being schooled in the basics of third-worldliness. Uniforms of sleeveless, torn, tank tops and bleach-stained jeans dress them in acceptance. Empty buckets swing from limp fingers waiting to be filled with clean water. The men must decide how to meet the demands of filth and thirst, kids and wives, and self with portioned allowance.

They will carry the buckets carefully back to their tents, their campers, the beds of semi trucks and storage units, their cots and sleeping bags and musty mattresses. They will divide the water into pots over open flames, boil Ramen in it, stain it with tea and instant coffee and infant formula, dip their hands and wash their faces. It will be soiled come morning, and they will taste destitution once again. They will be angry and frustrated for not having mastered the lesson of rationing, for not having been prepared for the worst, because surely this is the worst. Surely this is the bottom. Their faces say it; scream it as they look away from the camera. "We have nowhere to go but up," they said, "What more can we lose?" And God answered. He took their marriages, their youth, their jobs, their industry, their sobriety. The men were left with running water, and soft beds, and quite homes, the women with armfuls of babies and tender cheekbones.

My mother shoves me from the photo. "Can you not hear the goddamn baby crying?" she asks, unpeeling him from of my side and turning hard through the automatic doors. She is still clutching the check in her hand, and I know that we are not prepared for anything.

■ ■ ■

I am seventeen, sitting on a braided rug in my mother's living room, watching people spill out around the Superdome like ants. The television flashes with housetops peaking out of a great body of water. Oak trees float down highways like twigs in a gutter. Families crowd atop roofs and wave their broken wings. It is as if the perpetrator of a great assault has walked through the door and demanded that I look him in the face, and I do. I cannot look away.

For more than a decade we held the Trophy of Broken Homes. Hurricane Andrew was the most devastating storm to have ever hit the U.S., and we survived it. For years we reminded school reformers, social workers, and building inspectors of the damage left behind. "Look," we'd plead, waving a collage of before and after photos, divorce certificates, and eviction notices, "look what we've been through." Watching the screen, I realize that we are, again, displaced. No longer entitled to wallow in poverty, or inherit Section 8 housing with victimized reticence. Now we must be mobile, for the light shines on a fresher wound. The lens has refocused, and by God the people of New Orleans are drowning in their own shit.

My mother leans over a cold cup of coffee and rubs her temples. The babies are not babies anymore. They stand in front of the television screen and demand to know when they can watch Nickelodeon. They are dumb to the history that is unfolding within their own story. They are products of natural disaster, their cells fused under gaping holes in a collapsed ceiling. "Go to your room," my mother tells them. The youngest swears and slams his bedroom door.

The mayor is convinced that the storm has passed, that the water will recede and everyone will go back to their homes and rebuild. "We will rebuild," the residents say over and over, their faces swollen with emotion and defiance. I look at my mother and know that she is watching this disaster unfold through seasoned eyes. It is one of the few things we both understand. There will be no rebuilding.

The news anchors call the storm a monster, but they are mistaken. When the waters recede and the looting begins, when the sexual battery ripples through the campsites, when the FEMA checks run dry, and the rain turns to whiskey that is when the monsters wash up on shore. The real storm is still brewing, gaining traction in the pulse of blooming poverty. And when it makes landfall, no one will be watching.

■ ■ ■

I am five-years old, standing on the splinters of a swing set. My oldest sister is squatting over a five-gallon bucket humming the Sesame Street theme song, pissing. We are not to leave each other's side. She is slow and whiney, crying when we find baby dolls that are broken beyond repair. She spends the evenings rubbing the dolls' cheeks with my father's hanky. Sitting with my mother in our tent, she brushes their tangled hair and adjusts their ratty clothes.

I'm looking for marbles. The houses have all collapsed, and with them, jars and jars of marbles have been shattered, their contents rolling and lost amongst the debris. "It's your job to find them," my Dad says to me, "because when we rebuild and everyone comes back, the children are going to want to know what happened to their marbles." And I'll have them all. I'll hand the jars back to the children one-by-one as the families file past me to their new homes. So far I've found six. They clink together in the plastic grocery bag slung over my shoulder.

It's a dangerous job looking for marbles and baby dolls. Nails and glass form terrain children's shoes weren't meant to endure. We're not to wander too far from the tents. We're not to touch any animals. Should a dog approach us, we are to yell at it, kick it if we must, and come straight back to tell the adults. Against my mother's objection, I've been given a pocketknife. We haven't received our shots yet. Talks of tetanus and rabies have circulated through camp.

Across the rubble, the frame of a two-story house stands tall. Shooting up from a sea of splintered lumber and crumbled walls, it is defiant against the cloud-torn August sky. The garage door swings on a solitary creaking hinge like a white flag of surrender. I clamber through the jungle of drywall and rebar to meet the longest shadow I've stood under in days. The roof is gone, lost amongst thousands of shingles littering the yard. Fiberglass hangs from the rafters like a torn web, still dripping with coastal rain.

In the distance, I can hear my sister calling me. Her voice echoes off the cement piles, looking for a soft place to land. She does not want to be alone in the rubble. She is afraid of getting trapped in the labyrinth of debris. She is afraid of the dogs, the wind, the clouds that won't leave. I can hear the panic in her voice. Walls are still collapsing. We've heard them at night from our tents. The stillness of the earth will crack in the distance, and another house will fall. My mother has warned us of these houses, the ones that seem to have endured the worst. "They are the weakest," she says. Their frames are fractured. They will be bulldozed and rebuilt from nothing. Stay away from them, we're warned.

The house is open, gaping, caged only by ribs of steel and concrete. I fumble up the three steps leading to the mouth of the house and stand at the threshold. The plastic grocery bag of marbles flutters under my arm like a trapped bird. The floor is impenetrable, lined with waterlogged clothes, swollen fragments of furniture, and shreds of snowy insulation. Something is rotting nearby. I rub my shoe across the entrance, clearing a thick skin of dust off the broken tile. I trace a foot-long circle in the grime, reach my hand in the bag, drop the marbles into the circle, and begin to play. ■

GLADE CREEK FALLS

In a canyon of the Gorge
prills Glade Creek Falls—
beholden, as is proper, to the New.

Only the Nile is older.
Obscenely young, prey to impulse,
we indenture to the Glade—

our trysting place—and to each other.
Like the Bible, like Mythography,
we truss, foretold, in writ scrolls of eternity.

True love among children
is psilocybin; what we eat wild
from this earth claims us.

Outcroppings lounge in cloud mantles.
The water attempts modesty,
but may not veil itself.

It sprays from its secret cave,
evanescent, quicksilver. Twisted
Hemlocks screw into bedrock.

Poplars loose leaves over deep green pools.
The sun is barred, but for shadow, mottled.
On a fainting couch of rock

we strike our troth. Yet
whelped as I am in the quaking red
syllables of Gospel, Fayette County,

I know sin is black as bituminous.
Just so, I remain my Savior's primal witness.
The world hatches, named and fabled.

JOSEPH BATHANTI

BOOK REVIEWS

Helen Morales. *Pilgrimage to Dollywood: A Country Music Road Trip through Tennessee.* Chicago, Il.: University of Chicago Press, 2014. 192 pages. Hardcover. $22.50.

Reviewed by Elizabeth Glass

The travelogue *Pilgrimage to Dollywood* by Helen Morales is an enjoyable book for academics, intellectuals, and readers who love Dolly Parton, if they are able to overlook some unpleasantness that could offend a number of Southern readers. All of that may seem a strange combination, but for that niche audience who loves learning, Dolly Parton, and is willing to forgive judgmental tones at times, it is a pleasurable tale.

Pilgrimage to Dollywood opens with Morales at the annual "Dolly Homecoming Parade" in Pigeon

Forge. While Morales, a classicist educated at Cambridge who teaches at the University of California-Santa Barbara, enjoys the parade, she laments that academics don't think well of Dolly Parton or country music in general. She grew up listening to country music in England where her father had immigrated a teenager and became a fan of Parton's songs. He worked in restaurants when Morales was a child, and whenever Parton came on the radio in the kitchens, he told her, "This is our music"—working class music.

Her trip to the Nashville Parthenon is so engaging and inspiring it makes the reader want to jump in the car and drive there immediately. Morales describes that when she viewed the statue of the goddess Athena, for whom her daughter is named, "the hairs on the back of my neck stood up; I almost wet myself; I was rooted to the spot and stood gape-mouthed." It is the most real moment in the book, a place where she loses herself, becomes a tourist, and allows pure enjoyment. For her, the statue "surpasses any ancient description or extant image of a statue of Athena." Morales writes that the ancient Greeks believed gods can inhabit such statues, and that Nashville's Athena gave her an "understanding of this and of epiphany: the god manifest on earth."

Despite her love for this place and statue, she mars the description by including that her husband said, "[t]here'll be no twanging there," which seems to indicate Southerners would neither understand nor appreciate something so grand, in spite of Nashville having been labeled the "Athens of the South." This tone is present throughout the book, which makes it impossible to lose one's self in the tale; by quoting her husband's statement within the magnificent description of the Parthenon, Morales gives it weight, as if in tacit agreement with his assessment.

Similarly, the academic tone will alienate many travelogue and Dolly Parton fans. While Morales describes being in

Pigeon Forge waiting for the evening parade, she takes the reader away from the moment to give historical facts about what a pilgrimage is. This sort of scholarly explanation appears throughout the book, which makes serious what might otherwise be a fun trip to Dollywood and other country music attractions.

When Morales goes to Graceland, she expects to enjoy it, but finds that "the stiffness of the costumes on the headless

It is at Dollywood, though, where Morales is reminded of her love for Parton. She writes of the touches of Dolly throughout the park.

manikins could hardly contrast more strongly with the dynamism and energy" of Elvis. She's disappointed by the sanitized and commercialized version of Presley because there aren't pictures of his later years or anything regarding the problems that surrounded him. She writes that this idealized version of him takes much of the magic and power out of the man who was Elvis.

She has a much different view of Loretta Lynn's Coal Miner's Daughter Museum. She writes that it's the "oddest" museum she has ever visited, noting that while some of the placards and labels are professionally done, others are handwritten in felt-tipped pin with homespun notes on them signed "LL" and "Loretta Lynn." Although Morales states she is impressed by this, writing that it would an improvement if employed at the British Museum or New York Metropolitan Museum of Art, it is overshadowed when she points out that there are "elementary spelling errors" such as "to" for "too" throughout the notes.

Morales then visits the Country Music Hall of Fame, which she finds a glossy advertisement rather than a real look at what country music is and can be. She and her family travel to Gatlinburg, which she writes, "screamed fun in a way that the worthy-but-dull holiday destinations of my childhood, National Trust cottages in the grounds of English stately homes," did not. Though she writes she is "secretly thrilled" by this, again she comes across as disapproving of it.

When she goes back to Pigeon Forge, she and her family have dinner at Dolly Parton's Dixie Stampede Dinner Attraction. Morales enjoys the pre-show experience in which servers dress in antebellum attire and serve non-alcoholic cocktails. She disdains the dinner theater itself, though, because of the sanitized version of the Civil War, which does not depict the horrors of slavery and reality of battles. After this, Morales feels "alienation" from Dolly Parton, whom she had "so long admired.". Morales's reaction might be what many would have to the show, but the way she writes it makes it seem as if she's critical of Southerners rather than of these issues with the show.

When she visits Dollywood the following day, Morales writes she has "never seen so many fat people together in one place. So many unrepentant fat people, dressed in Capri pants and sleeveless tops". Though she notes that she fit right in and is a large woman herself, she is clearly judgmental, which seems, again, to flow against the book being for Dolly Parton fans who would enjoy a travelogue about going to Dollywood.

It is at Dollywood, though, where Morales is reminded of her love for Parton. She writes of the touches of Dolly throughout the park. Her daughter loves the rides, and Morales enjoys the history and the Chasing Rainbows Museum, which exists as a sort of biography of Parton. Morales is dismayed, though, by the notes written by Parton, signed "Dolly" throughout the Museum, and wonders who "borrowed" the idea from whom—Dolly or Loretta—not allowing that each woman may have come up with the idea for signing notes in her museum on her own.

When reflecting on her trip, her pilgrimage, when she is back home in California, Morales reads an interview in which Parton recounts that "'a lot of times my fans don't come to see me be me. They come to see me be them'". In spite of the disenchantment Morales felt toward Parton after going to the Dixie Stampede dinner theater, she writes that the "delight and gratitude [she] felt in Dollywood seemed earned. It is not that the journey is its own reward, but that the journey affects how you experience the destinations". In that, she finds, the pilgrimage was worth it, since it was a search for self-knowledge, which she has found.

Morales's writing is superb, and much of the book is gratifying, but the tone *Pilgrimage to Dollywood* may turn readers away.This can best be summed up when Morales writes, "Am I white trash? When I asked this question of my friend David, he laughed and said, 'Helen, you've been reading the National Enquirer for the last fifteen years.' So I have, but I've also been reading the Times Literary Supplement". To many, wondering if one is "white trash" isn't something to be bandied around and laughed at, but is instead a deep insult to the working class values that Morales says she espouses. It is this attitude that, while the book is quite pleasing in many aspects, could lead a reader to conclude that the author instead derides country music, and the people and places in the South. ■

PRUNUS AVIUM

Graceful eating it is not—
you must have muscle, desire
an adroit tongue that twists

and slides the pit to one side
as teeth separate sweet meat.
Do you spit before or after

summer explodes in your mouth?
The contemplative strips
every flesh-bit from the pit,

until as smooth as a river stone
while fingertips seek
the firmest in the bowl

ever thankful
for the fleshy drupe
and its staining juice.

ROSEMARY RHODES ROYSTON

BIRD WATCHING

The honest pigeon feels sick in the morning,
    the news unhappy, head aching from the night

before, awoken by what at first felt like joy
    but turned into dread as soon as it bubbled up

from that unappreciated darkness where
    she was used. The forgotten canary can

only dream about being noticed, purpose
    forgotten. He might as well be an Easter

bunny, as neglected as a risen Lord
    every other day of the year but Christmas

unless he's being blamed for singing, which he
    does best and reflexively. Never mind the

crow, intelligent but ever discontent,
    constant reminder of innocence gone for

ever, lifting off the carrion on the
    road into a sky flat as asphalt, part of

the scenery, the inevitable. And
    the uselessness of the dove! Dependent on

circumstances which have nothing to do with
    him and which are beyond his control. Out in

front, he can't decide, has no defense, the whole
    world an ark ever since the flood, surviving

afloat in space, supporting a few olive
    branches for plucking if they aren't stripped of leaves

in some camp, the most current means of stabling
    animals, two by two no longer possible.

SANDRA KOLANKIEWICZ

CONTRIBUTORS

Joseph Bathanti is former Poet Laureate of North Carolina and the award-winning author of eight books of poetry, the novels *East Liberty* and *Coventry*, a book of stories titled *The High Heart*, and two books of nonfiction titled *They Changed the State: The Legacy of North Carolina's Visiting Artists, 1971-1995* and *Half of What I Say is Meaningless*. A new novel, *The Life of the World to Come*, is forthcoming.

Amy Clark's writing has appeared or is forthcoming in *The New York Times*, NPR, *Still*, *Appalachian Heritage*, *Blue Ridge Country*, *Appalachian Journal*, and many others. Her co-edited book, *Talking Appalachian: Voice, Identity, and Community*, was used as a dialect resource for actors during the filming of *Big Stone Gap*, a movie adaptation of Adriana Trigiani's novel of the same title.

Jordan Farmer is originally from Logan, West Virginia, and is currently a Ph.D. student studying creative writing at the University of Nebraska-Lincoln where he teaches 20th Century Fiction and Creative Writing. His fiction has been a finalist of both the *Sycamore Review* Wabash Fiction Prize and *Cutbank*'s Montana Prize in Fiction. His writing has appeared in or is forthcoming in *The Southwest Review*, *Southern Humanities Review*, *Kestrel*, and *Rip Rap Journal*.

Elizabeth Glass holds Masters degrees in Creative Writing and Counseling Psychology. She received an Emerging Artist Award in Literary Arts from the Kentucky Arts Council, and a grant from the Kentucky Foundation for Women. Her writing has appeared in *Still: The Journal*, *River Teeth's* "Beautiful Things" series, *New Plains Review*, *Writer's Digest*, *The Chattahoochee Review*, and other journals. She lives in Louisville, Kentucky.

Angel Sands Gunn lives in Charlottesville, Virginia, with her husband and two daughters. Her work can be found on *Full Grown People*, *Literary Mama*, *The Voices Project*, and *Edible Blue Ridge Magazine*. She is working on a novel about a West Virginia family during the Great Depression.

Marc Harshman is the author of the poetry collection, *Green-Silver and Silent* and *All That Feeds Us: The West Virginia Poems.* His periodical publications include *The Georgia Review, The Progressive, Roanoke Review, Bayou,* and *Shenandoah.* His eleven children's books include *The Storm,* and three new children's titles are forthcoming. Marc is the poet laureate of West Virginia and lives in Wheeling.

Thomas Alan Holmes, a member of the East Tennessee State University English faculty, lives and writes in Johnson City. Some of his work has appeared in *Louisiana Literature, Valparaiso Poetry Review, The Connecticut Review,* and *The Southern Poetry Anthology Volume VI: Tennessee,* with poems forthcoming in *North American Review* and *Still: The Journal.*

Barbara Kingsolver's work has been translated into more than twenty languages. She was awarded the National Humanities Medal, received the 2011 Dayton Literary Peace Prize for the body of her work, and in 2010 won Britain's Orange Prize for *The Lacuna.* Her novel *The Poisonwood Bible* was a finalist for the Pulitzer Prize. She lives with her family on a farm in southern Appalachia.

Sandra Kolankiewicz's poems and stories have appeared most recently in *New World Writing, Gargoyle, Fifth Wednesday, Prick of the Spindle, Per Contra,* and *Pif.* Years ago, story of mine appeared in Appalachian Heritage. Her chapbook *Turning Inside Out* won the Black River Prize at Black Lawrence Press, and her chapbook *The Way You Will Go* is forthcoming from Finishing Line Press.

Erica Langston grew up in Homestead, Florida, a sinking town cradled between the Everglades and a nuclear power plant. Her childhood was loud, and greatly defined by siblings, storms, swamps and shallow graves. She is a graduate of the University of Florida, a 2011-2013 Fulbright Scholar, and an MSc candidate in Environmental Studies at the University of Montana.

Rosemary Rhodes Royston, author of *Splitting the Soil* (Finishing Line Press, 2014), resides in northeast Georgia. Her poetry has been published in journals such as *Southern Poetry Review, NANO Fiction, The Comstock Review, Main Street Rag, Coal Hill Review, Flycatcher, Still: The Journal, Town Creek Review,* and *Alehouse.*

Lauren Stonestreet is a photographer and creative director originally from West Virginia and currently based in Charlottesville, Virginia. She has worked with multiple publications across the country and abroad on assignment with companies and nonprofit organizations, and photographing dance and theatre companies. She enjoys being on the road and exploring and documenting her native Appalachia. For more about Lauren and her work visit www.elleeffect.com.

Larry D. Thacker's poetry can be found in past issues of *Still: The Journal; The Emancipator; Motif 2; Full of Crow; Kudzu Literary Magazine; Country Grind; The Southern Poetry Anthology, Volume VI: Tennessee; Mojave River Review;* and *Appalachian Heritage*. He is the author of *Mountain Mysteries: The Mystic Traditions of Appalachia* and the poetry chapbook, *Voice Hunting*. He serves as Associate Dean of Students at Lincoln Memorial University.

Crystal Wilkinson is the author of *Blackberries, Blackberries,* winner of the 2002 Chaffin Award for Appalachian Literature and *Water Street,* a finalist for both the UK's Orange Prize for Fiction and the Hurston/Wright Legacy Award. Her third book, a novel titled *The Birds of Opulence,* is currently with her agent Erin Cox and is under consideration. In 2014 she was appointed Appalachian Writer-in-Residence at Berea College.

Annie Woodford is originally from Henry County, Virginia. A graduate of Hollins College's MA program in Creative Writing, she now lives in Roanoke City, Virginia and teaches developmental English at Virginia Western Community College.

Amy Wright is the nonfiction editor of *Zone 3 Press,* and the author of four chapbooks. Her work can also be found in *Bellingham Review, Brevity, Drunken Boat, Quarterly West, Southern Poetry Anthology (Volumes III and VI),* and *Tupelo Quarterly*. She teaches at Austin Peay State University and resides in Tennessee, whose beautiful, defensible waterways help her current project, *Creeks of the Upper South,* written in collaboration with William Wright.